CW00541990

MAGNIFICENCE OF THE TSARS

CEREMONIAL MEN'S DRESS OF
THE RUSSIAN IMPERIAL COURT, 1721–1917
FROM THE COLLECTION
OF THE MOSCOW KREMLIN MUSEUMS

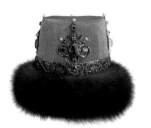

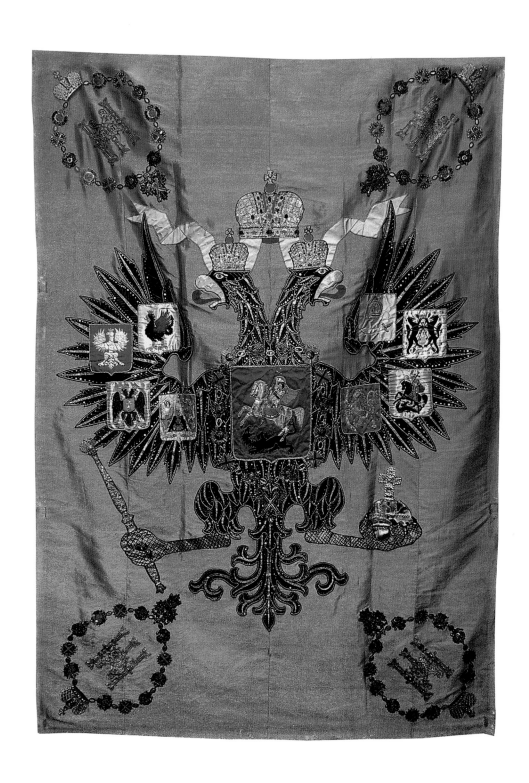

MAGNIFICENCE OF THE TSARS

CEREMONIAL MEN'S DRESS
OF THE RUSSIAN IMPERIAL COURT, 1721–1917

FROM THE COLLECTION
OF THE MOSCOW KREMLIN MUSEUMS

SVETLANA A. AMELEKHINA AND ALEXEY K. LEVYKIN
INTRODUCTION BY ROSALIND P. BLAKESLEY

V&A PUBLISHING

First published by V&A Publishing, 2008
V&A Publishing
Victoria and Albert Museum
South Kensington
London SW7 2RL

Distributed in North America by Harry N. Abrams, Inc., New York

ISBN 978 1 85177 550 7
Library of Congress Control Number 2008924019

10 9 8 7 6 5 4 3 2 1
2012 2011 2010 2009 2008

Designer: Price Watkins
Copy-editor: Slaney Begley
Original translation: Amanda Love Darragh

The objects are the property of The State Historical–Cultural Museum-Preserve
'The Moscow Kremlin'.
Unless otherwise stated, all photography of the objects is by the State Historical–Cultural
Museum-Preserve 'The Moscow Kremlin'.

Front jacket illustration: Red wool coat, 1727–30 (pp.58–9).
Back jacket illustration: Detail of sleeve from fancy dress costume of
Nicholas II, 1903 (pp.103–5).
Jacket flap: Boots, Coronation Herald's livery, 19th century (p.30).
Half-title: Hat from fancy dress costume of Nicholas II, 1903 (pp.103–5).
Frontispiece: Coronation canopy, 1896 (p.46).

Printed in Hong Kong

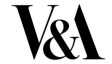

V&A Publishing
Victoria and Albert Museum
South Kensington
London SW7 2RL
www.vam.ac.uk

Contents

ACKNOWLEDGEMENTS

This book accompanies the exhibition *Magnificence of the Tsars* (December 2008–March 2009) at the Victoria and Albert Museum, London. The V&A is grateful to many people for their role in the exhibition and the book. In particular, we would like to express our gratitude to the many members of staff at The Federal State Institute The State Historical-Cultural Museum-Preserve 'The Moscow Kremlin': its General Director, Dr. Elena Gagarina; Director of Research, Dr. Alexey Levykin; Chief Curator, Olga Mironova; Deputy Director for Exhibitions, Zelfira Tregulova; Head of the International Relations' Department, Anastasia Parshina and Senior Research Officer, Dr. Svetlana Amelekhina, whose knowledge of the court dress collection led to the exhibition concept and who prepared this book and the introductions to each section.

For editorial input and support, we are grateful to the Russian editor, Irina Pantykina, and photographers Viktor Seregin, Aleksandr Sushenok and Valentin Overchenko; at the V&A to the curatorial team, Clare Browne, Edwina Ehrman, Esther Ketskemety, Daniel Milford-Cottam, Lesley Miller, Susan North, Angus Patterson, Alexey Unku; to the Exhibitions team, Rebecca Lim, Linda Lloyd-Jones and Tina Manoli; to the Publishing team, Frances Ambler, Mary Butler, Clare Davis, Mark Eastment and Clare Taylor; and for the original translation to Amanda Love Darragh.

NOTES ON THE TEXT

The specialist vocabulary of textiles and dress in the eighteenth and nineteenth centuries makes it extremely difficult to translate Russian directly into English for an audience not familiar with the nuances of Russian culture and society. Moreover, Russian adopted many words from foreign languages in this period, as well as retaining its own specific lexicon for traditional or folk items. We have therefore opted for terminology that is commonly used in reputable English-language fashion histories. The words used for military uniform derive from this vocabulary rather than from more specialist army literature, which has its own distinctions for dress. For those who are interested in the Russian terms, we have included an italicized transliteration in parenthesis after the English word in many cases on the first occasion that it occurs in the text. The transliteration of Russian follows a standard system, except where Russian Tsars' names are used in their English variants and where advised otherwise by the Kremlin. We have included a list of Further Reading after the Bibliography to enable enthusiastic readers to put this text into a broader Western European context. The Julian calendar has been used throughout.

Foreword

THE Moscow Kremlin Museums, including the Armoury Chamber, constitute Russia's oldest national Treasury and deserve to be well known in Great Britain. They celebrated their 200th anniversary in 2006. Their famous collections originated in the ancient hereditary property of Moscow's Emperors and Tsars and in the palace collections of the Russian Emperors; they include examples of the work of the most eminent master craftsmen of their day, whose creations rank amongst the most significant cultural artefacts worldwide. Symbols of power, objects of great value and historical rarities were created, carefully preserved and passed from generation to generation within the Kremlin. Distinguished by their originality, their exceptional artistic value and their technical perfection, these items are closely linked to some of the most famous figures and the most important events in Russian and world history.

Although Peter I moved the Russian capital to Saint Petersburg in 1712, the original capital, Moscow, with its treasure house safe within the Kremlin, remained the spiritual centre of the country and the place where Russian monarchs were crowned. From 1721 these monarchs bore the title of 'Emperor'. The Armoury enjoyed special status as the visible incarnation of Imperial wealth and power, and a number of new collections were established during the eighteenth century. One that we are particularly honoured to have in the Moscow Kremlin Museums is the collection of ceremonial court dress that dates from the eighteenth century to the beginning of the twentieth century. The highlight of the collection is the coronation attire of the Russian monarchs, which is unique in its commemorative significance and integrity. This collection of dress, most of which has never been exhibited before either in Russia or abroad, has only recently begun to be studied. It forms the basis of the exhibition *Magnificence of the Tsars: Ceremonial Men's Dress of the Russian Imperial Court, 1721–1917* and this accompanying book, and is presented here for the first time as a spectacular and significant expression of the culture of the Imperial Court.

After several years of serious and meticulous work on this project, we have selected over 100 objects to be shown to the British public. Gathered together for the first time in a single exhibition space, these items show the evolution of men's formal attire at the Russian Imperial Court. They are representative of the wealth and variety of ceremonial dress that has survived to this day in the Moscow Kremlin Museums. Only a small number of these articles are on permanent display in the rooms of the Armoury; the majority are kept in the museum's stores and have been specially conserved for this exhibition. By including costumes and accessories of the greatest historical and artistic significance, we have aimed to introduce the British public to the art of the finest dressmakers, tailors, embroiderers and jewellers working for the Russian Imperial Court; to the most spectacular examples of fashionable men's dress of the first third of the eighteenth century, made using expensive French plain and patterned silk and English wool, and decorated with the richest embroidery and lace; and also to the clothing worn by Knights of the Orders of Chivalry in the eighteenth century and the full dress uniforms of court officials at the end of the nineteenth century.

Visitors to this exhibition will be granted the unique opportunity to experience the legendary magnificence and luxury of the coronation ceremonies of Imperial Russia. Thanks to its location within the Moscow Kremlin, where coronation ceremonies traditionally took place, the Armoury Chamber had the exclusive right until the fall of the Russian monarchy to keep not only garments worn during the coronation ceremony but also the lavish ceremonial furnishings used in the Kremlin cathedrals and palace rooms and for ceremonial processions. Having survived wars and revolutions, these ceremonial furnishings now allow us to visualize the majestic surroundings that served as a luxurious backdrop to the monarchs' relatively modest coronation dress. Given the close family ties that existed between the Romanov dynasty and the British Royal Family, the complete collection of Russian Emperors' coronation dress, exhibited here for the first time, is bound to be of particular interest to the British public.

The relationship between Russia and Great Britain is based on firm and long-standing traditions, and *Magnificence of the Tsars* celebrates this unique connection. Part of a joint cultural exchange between the most prominent museums of Russia and Great Britain, it builds on many centuries of goodwill and a shared interest in the traditions and spiritual lives of our peoples.

These treasures from the very heart of Russia – the Moscow Kremlin – are an invaluable source of knowledge about bygone eras, and we hope that they will help to make the rich historical and artistic heritage of Russia more tangible and accessible to visitors of the exhibition.

Elena Gagarina
General Director of the Moscow Kremlin Museums

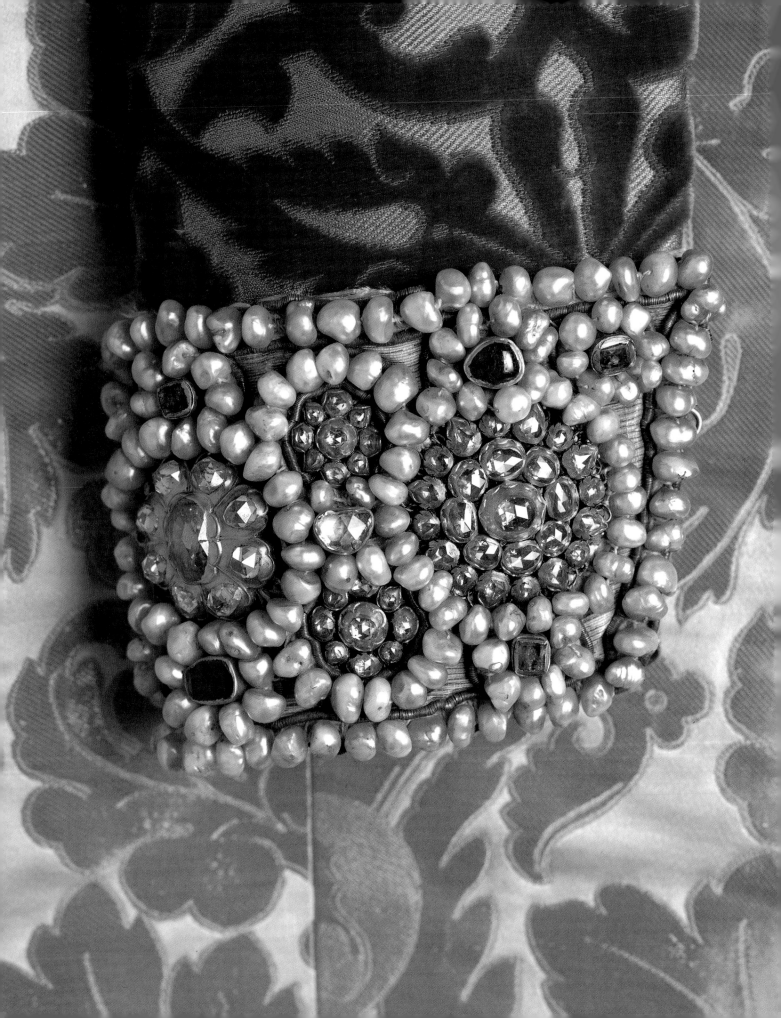

Introduction

ROSALIND P. BLAKESLEY

I N 1697, Tsar Peter I of Russia embarked on his first tour of Western Europe as part of a quest to modernize his country by emulating aspects of social, political and cultural life in the West. In the words of an early historian who drew on the Tsar's own 'campaign journals', Peter

> resolved to do something never done before by a [Tsar] … to leave his sovereign throne for the sake of seeing the most important European kingdoms, dominions, and regions, and to observe the various manners, customs, means of life, and forms of government. And to do this he created a Grand Embassy … which he himself accompanied incognito.[1]

The Tsar was entirely thwarted in his desire to travel incognito (Peter's extraordinary height of six foot seven inches, coupled with the fact that he was travelling with a retinue of 250 including dwarfs, trumpeters, musicians and surgeons, tended to give the game away). His determination to westernize his country, however, bore astonishing fruits, not least the city of Saint Petersburg, the Tsar's famous 'window on Europe', which was founded in 1703.

Yet just over two centuries later, the celebrated avant-garde artist Natalia Goncharova felt very differently about the role of Western Europe in her country's development, writing in an exhibition catalogue of 1913:

> Now I shake the dust from my feet and leave the West, considering its vulgarizing significance trivial and insignificant – my path is toward the source of all arts, the East. The art of my country is incomparably more profound and important than anything that I know in the West … I am opening up the East again, and I am certain that many will follow me along this path.[2]

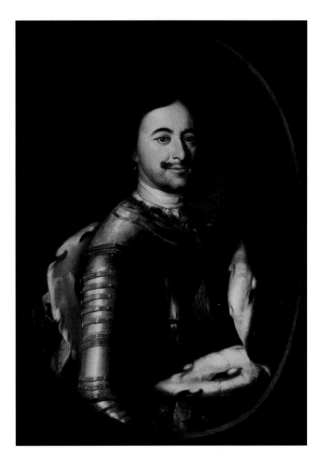

Portrait of Peter I (Peter the Great), unknown painter, 19th century. *Moscow Kremlin Museums.*

Opposite, detail of sleeve, Fancy Dress Costume of Nicholas II (see page 103)

The vehemence of Goncharova's sentiment points to the complexity of Russia's relationship with Western Europe. Memorably described by the writer Petr Chaadaev in 1836 as a country 'resting one elbow on China and the other on Germany',[3] Russia has continually sought to define its position vis-à-vis Western Europe, undergoing in the process centuries of intellectual rumination and self-analysis that have made an indelible impact on the history of Russian culture and design.

The reign of Peter I – the first ruler of Imperial Russia, having introduced the term 'Empire' in October 1721 – reveals how comprehensive the Tsar's vision of a new, westernized Russia was. Everything from the organization of the country's armed forces to the finest nuances of social etiquette was reconsidered in the light of information gleaned both from the personal experiences of Peter and his advisors abroad, and from the legion of foreign experts whom Peter recruited to work for the Russian court. Russia's administrative and tax systems were remodelled in accordance with Swedish precedent. A new Russian navy was founded, reflecting practices that Peter himself had observed in the shipyards of Holland and England. Overriding an edict issued by his father in 1675 forbidding courtiers to 'adopt the customs of the Germans and other foreigners, cut their hair, or wear dress, robes or hats of foreign design',[4] Peter insisted that members of Russia's élite should eschew traditional Russian clothes in favour of fashionable Western European attire. Even beards did not escape his notice: an order of 16 January 1705 decreed that all men should henceforth be clean-shaven, those objecting to such a practice being given the option of paying a fine the level of which depended on occupation and social rank. Such edicts were far from popular, particularly among those for whom a beard and whiskers were integral to their Orthodox faith:

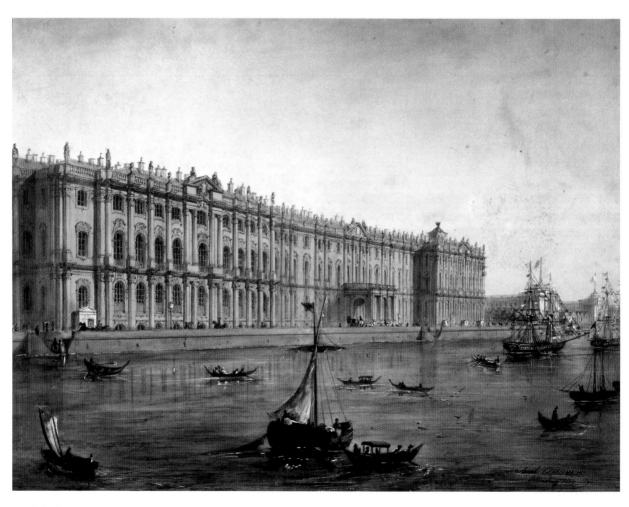

Iossif Charlemagne, *The Winter Palace from the Neva*, 1853.
State Hermitage Museum, Saint Petersburg.

in the words of the English ambassador Charles Whitworth, it was with great reluctance that they 'submitted to the Razor … their fore fathers lived unshaven, their priests, saints and martyrs were venerable for their beards … and the ignorant thought part of the devotion lay in the beard, as Samson's strength did in his hair.'⁵ Untroubled by such opposition, the Tsar pursued his path of westernization with ruthless efficiency, his legacy when he died in 1725 being a country whose structures of diplomacy, administration, defence and social organization were unrecognizable from those in place when Peter had ascended the throne in 1682.

Cultural and intellectual links with Western Europe continued to be fostered throughout the eighteenth century. Elizabeth Petrovna (reigned 1741–61), Peter I's daughter, commissioned the Italian architect Bartolomeo Rastrelli to redesign the Winter Palace in Saint Petersburg, cementing the tradition initiated by Peter of employing foreign artists and architects to embellish the new capital city and its surrounding palaces. Elizabeth's reign also saw the foundation of the Imperial Academy of Fine Arts (1757), which based its modes of tuition and student progression unequivocally on those of the Académie Royale de Peinture et de Sculpture in Paris. Moreover, for all of the rhetoric emphasizing the Academy's duty to educate Russian artists, ensuring that they received due professional recognition and remuneration, the first three artists invited to head its departments of painting, sculpture and printmaking were foreign. The faculty of architecture alone acknowledged that Russian practitioners might have come of age, and appointed Aleksandr Kokorinov to run an architectural class from 1758.

Priorities began to shift under Catherine the Great, whose accession represents one of the most remarkable episodes of Russian history. German by birth and education, Catherine seized the throne from her husband, Peter III, in a palace coup of 1762. Ever conscious of the unlawful route by which she had come to power, Catherine endeavoured to legitimize her position by applying her formidable energies and intellect to the development of Russia. Among her many achievements, the Empress presided over massive territorial gains for Russia, particularly in the south; she galvanized secondary and tertiary education (including provision for women); and she formalized proceedings at the Academy of Arts, granting the institution its formal charter in 1764. Yet for all her extraordinary contribution to the furtherance of Russia and her people, Catherine's sights remained firmly trained on the courts and cultures of Western Europe. The paintings with which she adorned the walls of her new Hermitage – an extension to the Win-

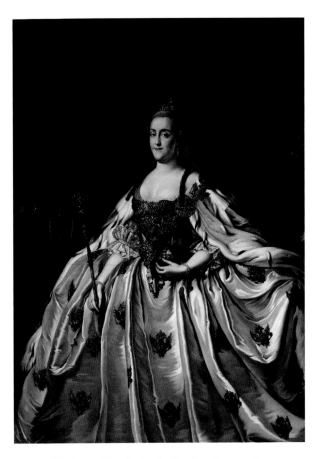

Portrait of Catherine II (Catherine the Great), unknown painter, 19th century. *Moscow Kremlin Museums.*

ter Palace from which she could retreat from the pomp and ceremony of court life – were by Western European, rather than Russian artists. The letters over which she laboured included extensive correspondence with Diderot and Voltaire. The artists and craftsmen whom she patronized featured some of Britain's finest, from Sir Joshua Reynolds to the Wedgwood porcelain manufactory. Even the equestrian statue (*The Copper Horseman*) that she commissioned in honour of Peter I was fashioned not by a Russian sculptor but by the Frenchman Étienne-Maurice Falconet and his pupil Marie-Anne Collot, who contributed the maquette for the head. Catherine may have been unquestionably devoted to Russia, but it was nevertheless inconceivable that her adopted country might choose to disassociate itself from those civilizations that lay to the West.

Such a state of affairs became subject to debate with the arrival of Napoleon and his formidable army, whose invasion of 1812 led to massive devastation and the burning of Moscow, until the Russian winter set in and the ill-prepared French troops were ignominiously driven from

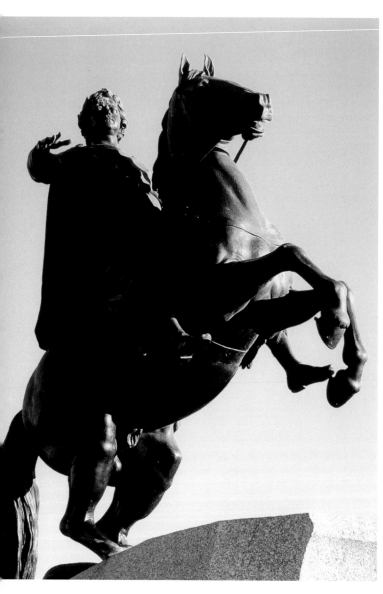

Étienne-Maurice Falconet and Marie-Anne Collot,
The Copper Horseman, Saint Petersburg, 1766–82.

Russian soil. Much has been made of the role of the Napoleonic War in fostering national pride in Russia, bringing a temporary halt to the Gallomania that had prevailed in the second half of the eighteenth century, and fostering instead a growing appreciation of the native Russian people or *narod*. Whatever the truth behind such interpretations, there is no doubt that the conflict caused Russians working in many different spheres to reassess their views of Western Europe. For example, in stark contrast to those academic painters obliged to emulate French painting in *la grande manière*, Russia's early caricaturists directly targeted the French in their work. Over 200 caricatures of Napoleon and his entourage appeared between 1812 and 1814, including Ivan Terebenev's biting image of *Napoleon in the Bathhouse*, in which the diminutive despot is subjected to the practice of beating with birch twigs, which continues to startle foreign visitors to Russian saunas to this day. Terebenev was strongly influenced by British satirists (he was occasionally referred to as 'the Russian Hogarth'), and he in turn was admired by the English caricaturist George Cruickshank. Thus, for all its impact on nationalistic debate, the Napoleonic campaign in no way curtailed cultural dialogue between Russia and Western Europe.

Over the following two decades, the vague patriotic sentiment that Napoleon's invasion had aroused gradually infiltrated official rhetoric, culminating in a ministerial circular of 2 April 1833 in which Sergei Uvarov, Nicholas I's minister of education, declared the three principles of Orthodoxy, Autocracy and Nationality – a triad that became know as Official Nationality – to be the foundation stones of Imperial rule. Russia's leaders had far from renounced all contact with Western European culture. Nicholas I, for example, inherited from his father, Paul I, a keen interest in military order and parade-ground fetish, and appointed the German painter Franz Krüger as official court artist to document the Russian army's manoeuvres and personnel. Nonetheless, the approved ideology of Nicholas' reign, rooted as it was in the practices of autocratic government, nationalism and the Orthodox Church, boasted an undeniably Russian authority.

As the century progressed, issues of national identity found expression too in numerous forms of cultural life. In literature, authors such as Ivan Turgenev drew on their personal experience of the Russian countryside to explore questions of social injustice and peasant welfare, most notably in *A Sportsman's Sketches*, a series of short stories that were published as a collected volume in 1852. In painting, the *Peredvizhniki*, a famous group of Realist artists founded in 1870, rejected the grandiose depiction of historical or mythical events advocated by the Academy in favour of more intimate images of everyday Russian life. In architecture, the Church of the Resurrection of Our Saviour on the Spilled Blood (1883–1907), which was erected to commemorate the spot where Tsar Alexander II was assassinated in 1881, deployed not the elegant neoclassical and Baroque forms for which Saint Petersburg is renowned, but the traditional domed constructions of Russian Orthodox churches (though interestingly its architect, Alfred Parland, was not Russian by birth). And in music, the five composers, including Modest Mussorgsky and Nikolai Rimsky-Korsakov, who became known as the Mighty Handful aimed to create a repertoire of pieces that reflected Russian musical forms such as village songs and church chants, rather than the influence of Italian opera and German lieder.

By the end of the century, so potent was the political currency of such associations with an identifiably Slavic heritage that Alexander III (reigned 1881–94) promulgated a formal policy of Russification that included, *inter alia*, expressing a growing interest in traditional Russian dress, and taking pains to sponsor a national school of art. Other members of the Imperial family followed suit, as when Nicholas II elected to wear a *kaftan* of gilt brocade and velvet to a masquerade in 1903 (see pp.103–5). In modelling his costume on fashions at the court of the late seventeenth-century Tsar Alexey Mikhailovich, whose style had been so comprehensively rejected by his son, Peter I, Nicholas signalled a clear identification with Russia's pre-Imperial past. Away from the restrictions of court etiquette, others were far more adventurous in how they chose to resurrect and reinterpret the material culture of the Russian *narod* or of Russia's Slavic and Byzantine heritage, as when Sergei Diaghilev stunned the cultural élite of Paris in the early twentieth century with the revolutionary theatre and costume designs of his Ballets Russes. The galaxy of artistic talents in Diaghilev's employ included Goncharova, who so evocatively rejected the 'vulgarizing significance' of the West as 'trivial and insignificant'. The time had dawned for Russian artists and designers to dominate the international stage.

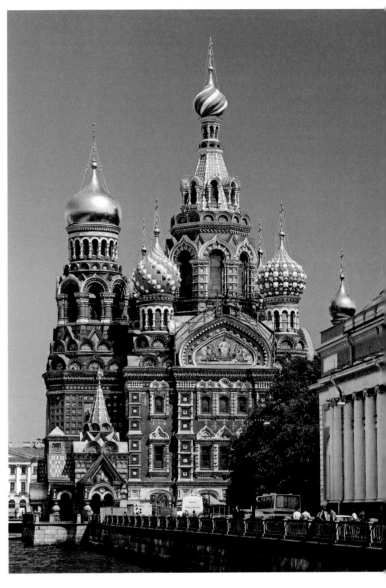

Alfred Parland, Church of the Resurrection of Our Saviour on the Spilled Blood, Saint Petersburg, 1883–1907.

Dress as a Reflection of Imperial Grandeur

SVETLANA AMELEKHINA

Out of the darkness of ignorance we have come onto the stage of glory before the entire world … we have been brought from non-being into being and have been included in the society of political nations.[1]

THE Moscow Kremlin is at the very heart of Russia, and the Museum-Treasury in its Armoury Chamber is where the commemorative collection of clothing belonging to the Russian rulers was formed. The oldest items in the collection come from the Treasury Court, which was where the Tsars' apparel was kept in the sixteenth and seventeenth centuries. This collection comprised a number of formal ceremonial outfits, whose symbolism was inspired by those of the Byzantine emperors. A contrasting group of Tsars' fashionable clothing in Eastern European style from the sovereign's court in the village of Preobrazhenskoye was added to the collection in 1705.

The intensive development of contacts with Western Europe at the end of the seventeenth century stimulated a transition in styles of dress. Borrowed from several countries, these fashions were described collectively in Russia as 'German dress.'[2] From 1690 onwards, Peter I (or Peter the Great, as he is better known outside Russia) wore this form of dress, made for him by Russian as well as foreign tailors. He also made purchases during his first visit (1697–8) to Western Europe. Between 1701 and 1724 he issued 17 decrees making Western European – 'Saxon and French' – dress compulsory for the urban population of Russia and regulating how it should be worn.[3] The gradual increase in the severity of punishment for failing to comply with these decrees testifies to the special role that Peter assigned to dress in the system of reforms taking place in the country.

On 22 October 1721 an event occurred that formally changed the political status of Russia: in celebration of the conclusion of the Treaty of Nystad, which represented a triumphant military victory for Russia, the Senate accorded Peter the title of 'Emperor'. The first Imperial coronation in the history of Russia – the crowning of Empress Catherine I, Peter's wife – took place in 1724. Pomp and ceremony in the original capital became a way to demonstrate the greatness of the new Empire, its wealth and its prosperity.

The coronation showed that Peter had transformed the image of the Tsar and the élite by creating his own new, Imperial style. Ladies were ordered to appear at the ceremony 'in a particular dress, called a *roba*, which was made from brocade with gold or silver embroidery, and gentlemen were expected to wear "lavish attire".'[4] A luxurious dress uniform, in green and red, was created for courtiers; it was the first time that this particular combination of colours was used. Thereafter, it became customary for staff of the Imperial Court to wear these colours.

From the moment the Treaty of Nystad was signed, Peter's wife and daughters set standards of elegance and good taste and the Emperor himself, who had hitherto been noted for his exceptional modesty, surprised foreign ambassadors by 'playing the dandy.'[5] He attended the Empress's coronation on 7 May 1724 in an ensemble made from 'sky-blue silk, embroidered with silver, wearing red silk stockings and a hat with a white feather,' and the Empress Catherine wore 'the richest of robes, made in the Spanish style, of purple damask with magnificent gold embroidery.'[6] Spanish court costume had come to symbolize the greatness of absolute monarchy and the purity of royal blood; thus, it was presumably no coincidence that it was the inspiration for the design of the coronation dress of the first Russian Empress.

A great deal of thought was also given to the choice of colour for the coronation ensembles of both the Empress and the Emperor. During the heyday of the Byzantine Empire, light blue and purple were symbolic of supreme power. In Byzantium gold was the colour of Imperial victory, and probably for this reason it was the colour chosen for Catherine's coronation mantle. This item of coronation regalia was entirely new in Russia. It was edged with ermine, a symbol of purity and integrity, and decorated with the new State Emblem of the Russian Empire, the two-headed eagle under the Imperial crown. A new mantle was made for every sub-

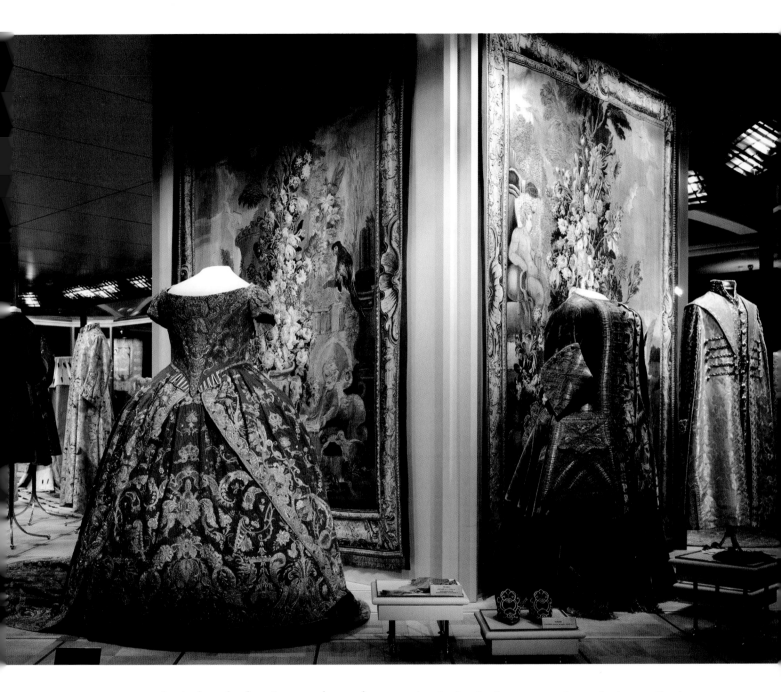

Display of 18th and 19th-century court dress in the Armoury Chamber, Moscow Kremlin Museums.

sequent coronation in the style of previous mantles – today 14 of them are housed in the Kremlin Museum.

After the coronation of Catherine I, the dress, gloves, stockings, shoes (*bashmaki*) and garters from her coronation outfit were given to the Armoury. The decision to keep them in the Treasury was almost certainly taken by the Emperor himself, who had become familiar with a number of collections of the coronation attire in other European courts during his foreign travels. Prior to Peter the Great's rule, the Tsar was traditionally buried covered with his

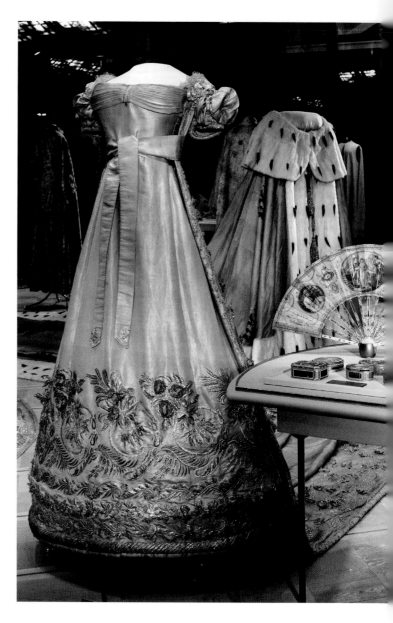

coronation robes. However, after Peter, all subsequent Russian monarchs gave their garments to the Treasury. As a result, the collection in the Armoury encompasses the entire Imperial period of Russian history, spanning 200 years.

Ceremonial dress, particularly coronation dress, opens the door to many aspects of the past. Its symbolism is not always clear to us, although it would have been obvious to anyone witnessing events at the time when absolute monarchies took every care to ensure that there could be no element of doubt or ambiguity in the messages relayed through the visual symbols they used. On 22 September 1770 an event took place that defined the style of ceremonial dress of the Russian Imperial Court until the end of its existence: on the anniversary of her coronation, Empress Catherine II (subsequently 'the Great') 'was pleased to attend a ball in Russian dress,'[7] which she subsequently wore for all official ceremonies. A highly educated witness to this event wittily remarked that she had worn it 'for physical, as much as political reasons.'[8] He was referring to the fact that the Empress did not have Russian roots but purposefully demonstrated her adherence to the traditional cultural values of her subjects, in whose name she had been accorded the title 'Mother of the Fatherland' in 1767. We believe that this title in turn is what led to the creation of an official ensemble for the Empress, corresponding to the traditional 'Russian dress' in symbolism and style. It remained her exclusive privilege until 30 August 1775. On that day, a number of female courtiers attended the feast day of one of the Russian orders in dresses of a similar style, and three months later, at Her Majesty's name-day celebrations, the remaining female courtiers followed suit.[9]

In June 1775, the Military School for the nobility had arranged a celebration in honour of the Empress on the conclusion of a peace treaty with Turkey, 'The Destruction of the Temple of Fashion' being an allegorical spectacle that was presented during the festivities. A comedy entitled 'Fashion, Whose Mask is Torn Off by the Genius of Love for the Fatherland' openly mocked the prevailing passion for French fashion, which had been adopted by the most distinguished families during the reign of Empress Eliza-

beth Petrovna. It was seen as ruinous for the State and Catherine the Great was still trying in vain to eradicate it. The performances were a huge success and were repeated several times in June 1775. The Empress's suppression of Western fashion went so far as dismissing and depriving of honorary posts those nobles who continued it. In response female courtiers abandoned their French fashions in favour of Russian-style attire, an imitation of the multi-layered, long-skirted dress of the upper classes of pre-eighteenth-century Russian society and of contemporary festive folk dress. The distinguishing features of this new 'Russian-style' court attire were the draped sleeves of the underdress, the hanging sleeves of the overdress, the way the dress was

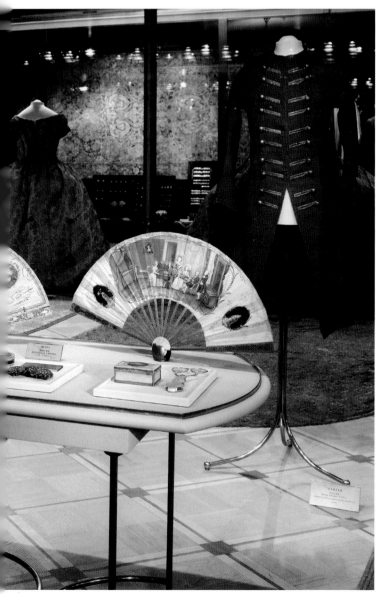

declared to be a 'return to ancient Russian origins'. The inclusion of traditional folk dress in court ceremonials demonstrated the national character of the monarchy. The symbolism used during the ceremony created an impression of the sovereigns as the 'embodiment of Russia', Europeanized court culture being complemented by national attributes. It has been suggested that national outfits were intended to make the Russian Imperial Court stand out from the rest of Europe and to demonstrate the unity of the Tsar and the Court with the people.

Later court festivities invariably made a great impression on European guests; the Bavarian envoy at the coronation of Nicholas II referred to what he witnessed as 'a stunning spectacle of the might and greatness of Russia.'[10] The main aim of such festivities was to overwhelm Western governments and society with the magnificence of the Russian monarchy, as well as to influence Russians themselves. In her memoirs one Maid of Honour expressed pride in her country's grandeur thus: 'Power in Russia is so pure and so majestic, whereas in other countries it remains in name alone: ours bears a religious and almost supernatural character, which excites the imagination.'[11]

shaped in front like a peasant shirt dress (*sarafan*), and the *kokoshnik* head-dress with veil. Although it underwent a whole series of modifications over time, this court dress, nicknamed by one contemporary 'the Frenchified *sarafan*', essentially remained the ceremonial uniform for female courtiers until the fall of the monarchy in 1917. From the beginning of the nineteenth century, it also became the customary coronation dress of the Russian Empresses.

Changes in men's court dress began to take place in the 1850s, in military as well as civil variants, as tail-coats were replaced by frock-coats. The cut gradually began to move towards that of men's national dress, reaching its most 'Russian' in the reign of Emperor Alexander III. It was

Emperors of the Romanov Dynasty

ALEXEY LEVYKIN

THE royal dynasty of the Romanovs ruled Russia from the seventeenth to the twentieth century. The Romanov roots can be traced to Andrei Kobyla, a landowner and nobleman who served at the court of the Muscovy Princes in the mid-14th century. His descendants included not only the Romanovs, but also many of Russia's most prominent noble families. The first Romanov Tsar was Mikhail Feodorovich, who ruled from 1613 to 1645. In 1721, in place of Muscovy Tsardom, the new Empire of Russia was established. Mikhail Feodorovich's grandson, Peter I, became its first Emperor.

All portraits of Emperors who ruled in the 18th century are 19th-century copies of the original portraits. They and the majority of portraits of the 19th-century Emperors were executed by unknown painters especially for the Armory Chamber. The miniature photo-portrait of Alexander III was made at the end of the 19th century by O'Connel, Paris. The miniature of Nicholas II was made by an unknown painter at the beginning of the 20th century.

PETER I (Peter the Great)
Tsar 1682–1721
Emperor 1721–5

Peter I was the 14th child of Tsar Alexey Mikhailovich, born on 30 May 1672 from his second marriage to Natalia Kirillovna Naryshkina. Having ruled jointly with his brother Ivan V from 1682, on Ivan's death in 1696 Peter was officially declared Sovereign of all Russia. He married twice and had 11 children, many of whom died in infancy. The eldest son from his first marriage, Tsarevich Alexey, was convicted of high treason by his father and secretly executed in 1718. Peter died from a chill on 28 January 1725 without nominating an heir. He was buried in the Cathedral of the Saint Peter and Saint Paul Fortress in Saint Petersburg.

During his reign Peter undertook extensive reforms: he created a regular army and navy, brought the Church under the control of the State, and introduced new administrative and territorial divisions in the country. He was a far-sighted and skilful diplomat and a talented military leader. Under Peter's rule Russia became a great European nation. In 1721 he was accorded the title of Emperor of All Russia, Great Father of the Fatherland and 'the Great', the title by which he is best known in Western Europe.

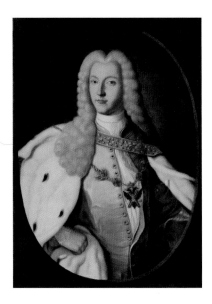

PETER II (Peter Alexeevich)
Emperor 1727–30

Grandson of Peter the Great and son of Tsarevich Alexey Petrovich from his marriage to Crown Princess Sofia Charlotta of Braunschweig-Wolfenbüttel, Peter II was born on 12 October 1715. After the death of

Catherine I in 1727 he ascended the throne at the age of 11. By order of Catherine, the State was to be ruled by the Supreme Privy Council with the participation of Tsarinas Anna Petrovna and Elizabeth Petrovna until he reached his majority. During the first year of Peter's reign, actual power was in the hands of his guardian, Peter the Great's former favourite, Prince A.D. Menshikov.

On 9 January 1728 Peter moved to Moscow with his court and the Supreme Privy Council. Here his coronation took place on 25 February in the Cathedral of the Assumption in the Kremlin. On 6 January 1730 he caught a chill, subsequently contracting smallpox. He died on 19 January 1730 and was buried in the Cathedral of the Archangel in the Kremlin.

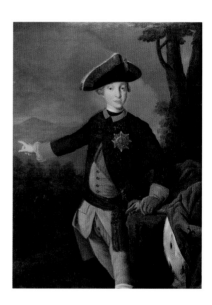

PETER III (Peter Feodorovich)
Emperor 1761–2

Son of Karl Friedrich, Duke of Holstein-Gottorp and Anna Petrovna, Peter the Great's daughter, Peter III was born on 10 February 1728 in Kila and christened Karl Peter Ulrich. He was proclaimed

official heir to the Russian throne on 7 November 1742 by his aunt Elizabeth Petrovna. On 21 August 1745 he married Princess Sophia Augusta Frederica of Anhalt-Zerbst, who was christened into the Orthodox faith as Catherine Alexeevna (later known as Catherine the Great) Peter ascended the Russian throne on 25 December 1761, the day Empress Elizabeth Petrovna died. His son later became Emperor Paul I. On 28 June 1762 he was overthrown by a court coup led by his wife. After his deposition he was imprisoned in Ropshinsky Castle, where on 7 July 1762 he was killed by Count Alexey Orlov, Catherine's favourite and one of the organizers of the coup. Peter was buried in the Annunciation Church of the Alexander Nevsky Monastery but in December 1796, by order of his son Paul I, his remains were reburied with full honours in the Cathedral of the Saint Peter and Saint Paul Fortress in Saint Petersburg.

During his short reign Peter III introduced various reforms, banned the persecution of dissenters, dissolved the Privy Council, and by special decree released the gentry from compulsory State service.

PAUL I (Pavel Petrovich)
Emperor 1796–1801

Son of Peter III and Catherine the Great, Paul was born on 20 September 1754 and brought up at the court of his great-aunt, Empress Elizabeth Petrovna, who intended to appoint him her heir. After the overthrow of Peter III he lived with his family in Gatchina Palace, given to him by his mother. He had his own court and a small army. Paul married twice and from his second

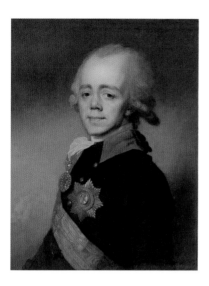

marriage in 1776 to Princess Sophia Dorothea of Württemberg (Maria Feodorovna), he had 10 children. On 6 November 1796, the day of Catherine the Great's death, the 42-year-old Paul declared himself Emperor. His reign was brief, for on the night of 12 March 1801 he was suffocated by conspirators. He was buried in the Cathedral of the Saint Peter and Saint Paul Fortress in Saint Petersburg.

Historians are equivocal about his reign. He was unpopular at court and extremely hostile towards his mother. His coronation signalled a break with the stability of Catherine's reign. Paul freed those imprisoned by the Privy Council, liberated the Poles, abolished conscription, and limited the power of landowners over their serfs. On 5 April 1797 he issued a decree on rights of succession that established procedures for the transfer of power from one monarch to the next. In foreign policy he performed an abrupt reversal in Russia's relationship with France, from war to union. It was probably this unpopular move that motivated his murder.

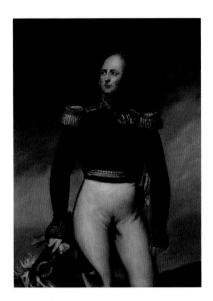

ALEXANDER I
(Alexander Pavlovich)
Emperor 1801–25

Eldest son of Emperor Paul I, Alexander was born on 12 December 1777. He came to the throne after the murder of his father on 12 March 1801, and was crowned in the Cathedral of the Assumption in the Moscow Kremlin on 15 September. Alexander died on 19 November 1825 in Taganrog and was buried in the Cathedral of the Saint Peter and Saint Paul Fortress in Saint Petersburg.

As a young Emperor, he was extremely popular among all levels of society, the first half of his reign being marked by a liberal internal policy. His various reforms included a restructuring of the country and an attempt to codify Russian legislation. Later, however, he reversed many of these changes.

NICHOLAS I (Nikolai Pavlovich)
Emperor 1825–55

The third son of Emperor Paul I, Nicholas was born on 25 June 1796. He came to the throne after the death of his elder brother Alexander I. He married Frederica Louisa Charlotta Wilhelmina (Alexandra Feodorovna), daughter of King Friedrich Wilhelm III of Prussia in 1817, and had seven children. He was crowned on 22 August 1826 in the Cathedral of the Assumption in the Moscow Kremlin. He died on 18 February 1855 and was buried in the Cathedral of the Saint Peter and Saint Paul Fortress in Saint Petersburg.

His reign saw the flourishing of absolute monarchy in both military and civil areas. He strengthened and centralized bureaucratic structures to an unprecedented degree. Harsh and despotic by nature, he suppressed brutally any sign of liberalism in Russia. The principal issue in foreign policy was the 'Eastern Question' – maintaining pro-Russian regimes in the Black Sea Straits. Nicholas attempted to resolve this by the partition of the Ottoman Empire. The result was the Crimean War of 1853–6, in which Russia suffered a bitter defeat at the hands of a coalition of Western European states and Turkey.

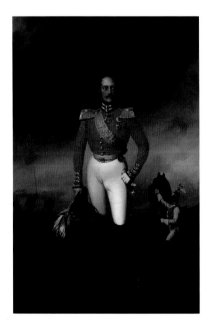

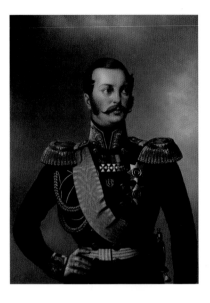

ALEXANDER II
(Alexander Nikolaevich)
Emperor 1855–81

Eldest son of Emperor Nicholas I, Alexander was born on 17 April 1818 and came to the throne on 19 February 1855 after the death of his father. He was crowned in the Cathedral of the Assumption in the Moscow Kremlin on 26 August 1856. From his marriage in 1841 to Maria of Hessen-Darmstadt (Maria Alexandrovna), he had seven children. On 1 March 1881 in Saint Petersburg he was mortally wounded by a bomb thrown by a student member of the revolutionary organisation 'The National Will'. The Church of the Resurrection of Our Saviour on Spilled Blood (see p.13) was erected on the site of the murder. He was buried in the Cathedral of the Saint Peter and Saint Paul Fortress in Saint Petersburg.

Alexander implemented important reforms in national, military and municipal organization, and notably the abolition of serfdom. He also rethought foreign policy: Russia now refrained from overseas expansion and concentrated on strengthening her borders. His greatest foreign policy achievement was the successful war of 1877–8 against the Ottoman Empire, resulting in the liberation of Bulgaria and the annulment of the conditions of the Treaty of Paris of 1856, which had marked Russia's defeat in the Crimean War.

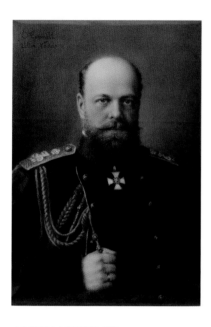

ALEXANDER III
(Alexander Alexandrovich)
Emperor 1881–94

The second son of Alexander II, born on 26 February 1845, Alexander III became official heir to the throne after the death of his elder brother Nicholas in 1865. From his marriage in 1866 to the Danish Princess Dagmar (Maria Feodorovna) he had six children. He came to the throne on 1 March 1881, at the age of 36, after the assassination of his father, and was crowned in the Cathedral of the Assumption in the Moscow Kremlin on 15 May 1883. He died on 20 October 1894 in Livadia, Crimea, and was buried in the Cathedral of the Saint Peter and Saint Paul Fortress in Saint Petersburg.

Alexander's reign coincided with an industrial revolution in Russia and the strengthening of capitalism. His domestic policy was particularly harsh, directed not only against revolutionaries but also other liberal movements. Fearing an attempt on his life, he refused to live in the Winter Palace; instead, he lived away from Saint Petersburg in Gatchina, his great-grandfather Paul I's palace.

NICHOLAS II
(Nikolai Alexandrovich)
Emperor 1894–1917

Nicholas II, the last Russian Emperor, was the eldest son of Alexander III, and was born on 6 May 1868. He ascended the throne after the death of his father on 20 October 1894, and was crowned on 14 May 1896. From his marriage in 1894 to the daughter of Grand Duke Ludwig of Hessen, Alice Victoria Eleanor Louisa Beatrice (Alexandra Feodorovna), grand-daughter of Queen Victoria, he had five children.

A stubborn supporter of the divine right of the sovereign, he did not give way on a single issue and struggled desperately to hold on to power during both the 1905 and 1917 revolutions. Freedoms accorded to the people in his manifesto of 17 October 1905 were soon withdrawn. In foreign policy, he took steps to stabilize the international situation, initiating two peace congresses at The Hague. During his reign Russia was involved in two wars. Loss of territory, massive casualties, and confusion at home were the main reasons for the Second Russian Revolution in February 1917. On 2 March 1917 Nicholas II abdicated. After the abdication the royal family first remained in Tsarskoe Selo then, by decision of the interim government, were transported to Tobolsk in Siberia. In April 1918 the Bolshevik government decided to move the Imperial family to Ekaterinburg in the Urals. Here they were all shot on 17 July 1918.

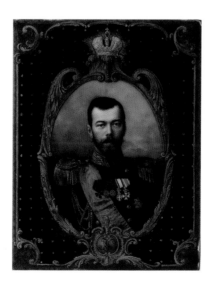

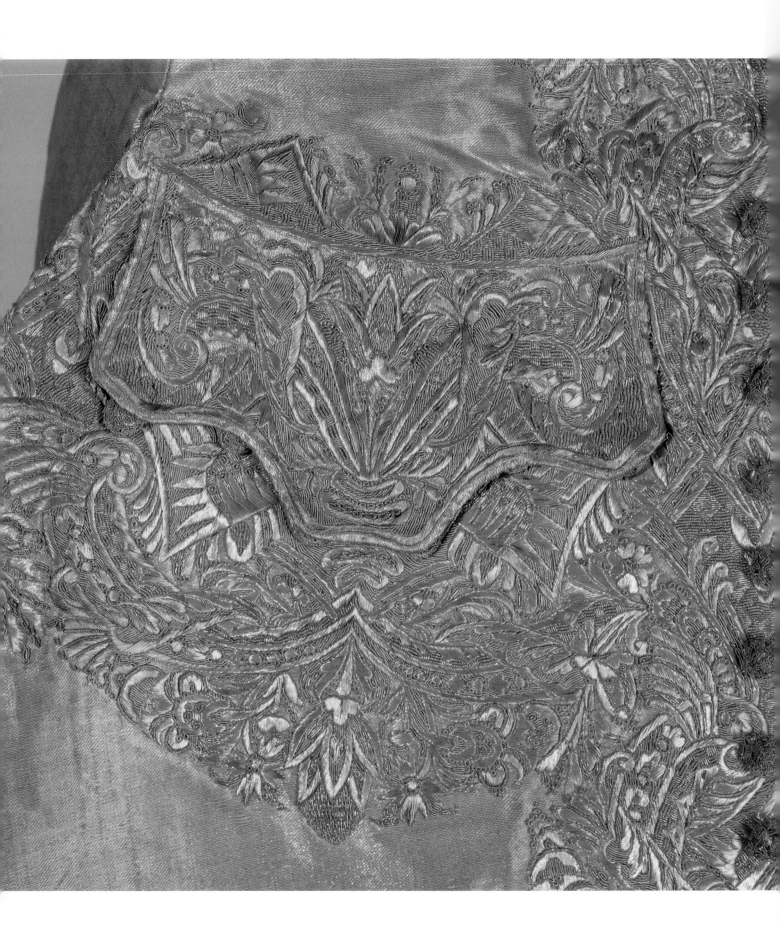

Coronations

[T]he coronation of Russian sovereigns, due to the setting and the immutability of its framework, which has come to support a powerful body, is … to its participants a spectacle incomparable with anything else in its gripping beauty and intrinsic meaning …
for these few hours alone it is possible to experience at once all the might, all the greatness of Russian Power….[1]

THE coronation ceremonies of Imperial Russia were remembered by not only witnesses but also direct participants as a 'magical dream'[2] reminiscent of 'a scene from a Wagner opera,'[3] and artists and writers recorded the most significant episodes of these majestic events for posterity. Today, more than a century after the last coronation in Russian history, the collection of coronation garments and ceremonial furnishings in the Moscow Kremlin Museums makes it possible to imagine the fairytale splendour of these celebrations. This collection was deliberately assembled over the course of two centuries in the Armoury Museum and ranks among the most significant coronation collections in Europe.

Peter the Great himself played an active role in developing the procedure for the Russian Imperial coronation ceremony. It united elements of ancient Russian consecration ceremonies, based on Byzantine tradition, and Western European coronation ceremonies from the late seventeenth century to the early eighteenth century. The ceremony required specific furnishings, which were created for the first time in 1724 with great care by the most skilled artists and decorators. They served as the standard for furnishings for the following 10 Russian coronations. Preparation for such coronations usually took about a year and was managed by a special Coronation Committee, which was allocated colossal sums of money from the State budget. Expensive fabrics and lace for decorating rooms in the palace and the cathedrals of the Kremlin were ordered abroad or made in Russian workshops; snow-white ermine for the coronation mantles and the throne canopies was transported from Siberia. The most eminent master craftsmen created the intricate embroidery and appliqué work that decorated the Emperor's coronation outfits and mantles and the coronation heralds' uniforms, as well as the enormous canopies, hangings behind the throne and wall hangings.

Each coronation ceremony led to the creation of a new outfit for the monarch in question. These clothes were worn by the anointed monarch only once and were treated with the same reverence as a sacred object. At the end of the festivities they were usually handed over to the Kremlin Treasury, where ten women's coronation dresses and seven men's ensembles are kept to this day. From the late eighteenth century onwards, Russian Emperors wore military uniform for their coronations. This uniform became a potent symbol of political superiority at a time when there was a somewhat romanticized view of war and when rulers were no longer idealized as divine beings.

Russian Emperors were particularly fond of military uniform and wore it almost exclusively, donning civilian dress only during foreign trips. Their magnificent full-dress uniforms projected elegance and luxury and martial authority. In the nineteenth century, many European monarchs adopted elaborate military uniforms for certain occasions, including Britain's King George IV, but the first sovereign to wear it for his coronation was the Russian Emperor Paul I in 1797.

Detail of coronation waistcoat
of Peter II, 1727 (see p.25).

CORONATION DRESS OF EMPEROR PETER II, 1727

Silk – Lyons (?)
TK-1935, TK-1936, TK-1937, TK-1938, TK-208/1-2, TK-202/1-2

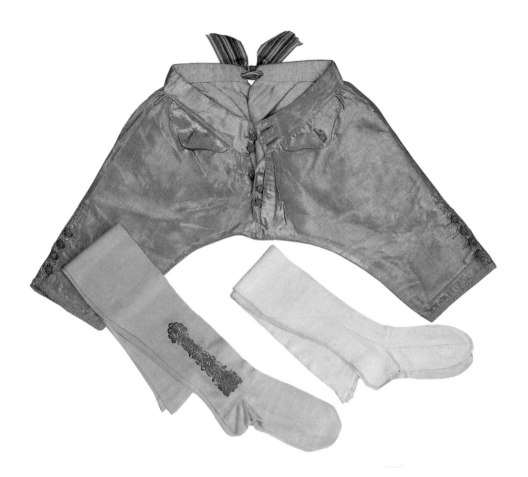

THE coronation of Peter II took place on 25 February 1728, and six months later by order of Vice-Chancellor A.I. Osterman the clothes worn by the young Emperor at the ceremony were handed over to the Armoury: a coat, waistcoat and breeches made from plain cloth of silver, embroidered with gold; a black felt hat with gold lace around the brim; drawers and shirt of 'Holland linen', with cravat and cuffs of 'German lace.'[4] For the coronation ceremony, the Emperor wore two pairs of stockings, either for warmth or possibly to make the legs look more shapely. The outer stockings, knitted from light-grey silk, coordinated perfectly with the rest of the outfit and were decorated with gilt embroidery. The second pair was made of thick white linen thread and was worn underneath the first.

This is the earliest Emperor's coronation ensemble in the Kremlin collection, and the only one cut in a fashionable Western European style. The tradition that it was made in France is corroborated in part by a report from the Spanish envoy to Russia. He wrote that the coronation was being postponed because the Emperor was still waiting for merchants to return from Lyons with fabrics and other goods that were to be used in the staging of the festivities.[5] An impression of extravagant, dazzling wealth is achieved by the combination of cloth of silver and the shimmering gold of the lavish embroidery, in which large ornamental motifs interlace with fantastical flowers and fruits. Imported plain cloth of silver was used in Russia for the creation of Tsars' attire from the seventeenth century onwards. In the eighteenth century it became known by the French terms *glacé* or *glazette*, and it was woven at a number of Russian silk-weaving workshops founded in Moscow during the reign of Peter the Great.

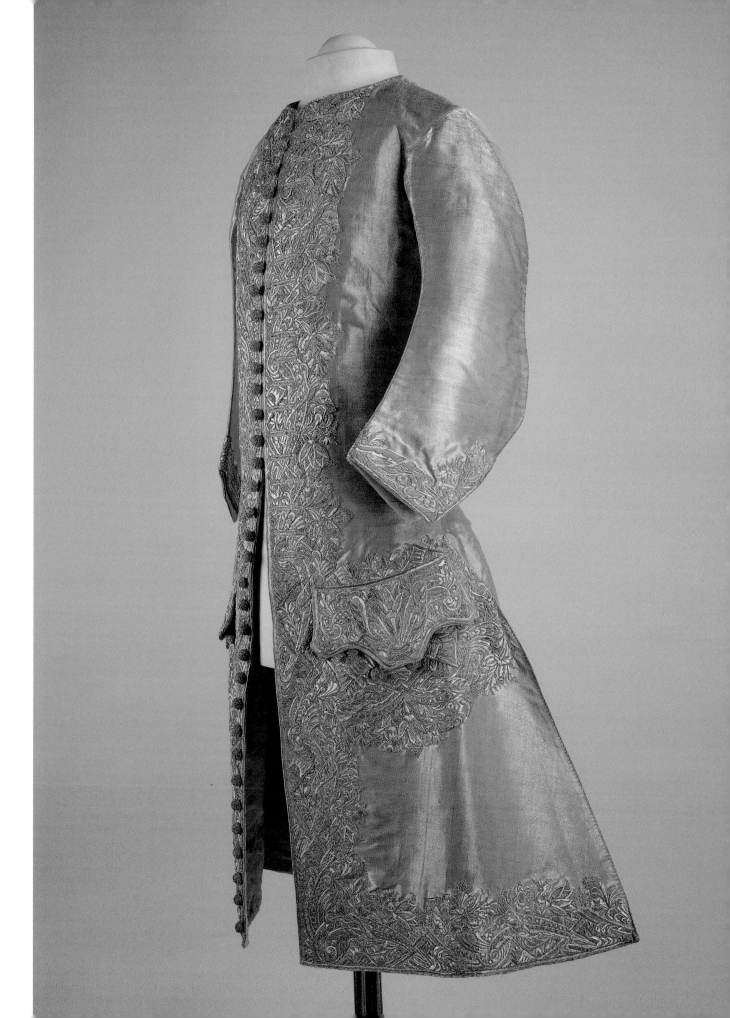

PART OF A CORONATION CANOPY, 1727

Russia
TK-3442/1-2

FOR the coronation ceremony in the Cathedral of the Assumption in the Moscow Kremlin, a canopy was suspended above the dais bearing the throne. It hung from tasselled gold cords and featured the embroidered coat of arms of the Russian Empire in the centre and the monogram of the monarch being crowned in each of the corners. Velvet panels were fastened to the sides of the frame, and the canopy was topped with a gilded metal cornice decorated with crowns, coats of arms and ostrich feathers.

Only a few coronation canopies were made in over two centuries of Imperial Russian rule; the first of these was made in 1724 by the French upholsterer Ivan Rozhbot for the coronation of Empress Catherine I. The velvet for this canopy was bought in Venice, and the various types of gilt braid came from France.[6] The canopy was probably reused at the coronation of Peter II, which took place only three years later. All that remains of the canopy of Peter II are the four horizontal panels from around the top and the decorative cords and tassels. The panels are made from red velvet and lined with taffeta. The edges are trimmed with wide gilt braid, and the centre of each features ornamental compositions in the form of garlands intertwined with ribbons and topped with crowns.

CUSHION FOR THE CROWN, 1762

Moscow
FABRIC — FRIEDRICH WILHELM NIKLAUS
FRINGE AND TASSELS — V. MAMONOV
TK-1290

THE Russian Imperial Regalia since 1742 include a crown, a sceptre, an orb, a chain of the Order of Saint Andrew, a mantle, and the State shield, sword, standard and seal. In 1798, a Lesser Imperial Crown, Lesser chain of the Order of Saint Andrew and mantle were added to this set, which was used for the crowning of the Emperor's wife. Part of the Regalia has always been kept in the Armoury in Moscow, and part was brought from the Imperial capital Saint Petersburg before each coronation.

The Imperial Regalia were treated like sacred objects. The coronation ceremony emphasized that role by not allowing anyone except the Emperor himself and the high priest to touch them. During the procession, the Regalia were carried by the highest court officials and their assistants on special cushions, which were made from cloth of gold and decorated with a fringe and tassels. The Regalia were then displayed on these cushions on a table in the Cathedral of the Assumption and were handed to the Emperor during the ceremony.

This cushion, which is the earliest example from the Armoury collection, was made to carry the Great Imperial Crown during the coronation of Catherine the Great. The fabric for the cushion was made in Moscow at the silk-weaving workshop of Friedrich Wilhelm Niklaus, a merchant of the first guild; the fringe and tassels were made in the workshop of the merchant V. Mamonov.[7]

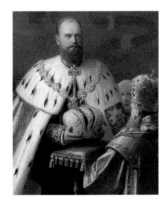

The coronation of Emperor Alexander III.
From the book 'Opisanie koronatsii imperatora Aleksandra III i imperatritsy Marii Feodorovny' (Saint Petersburg, 1885).

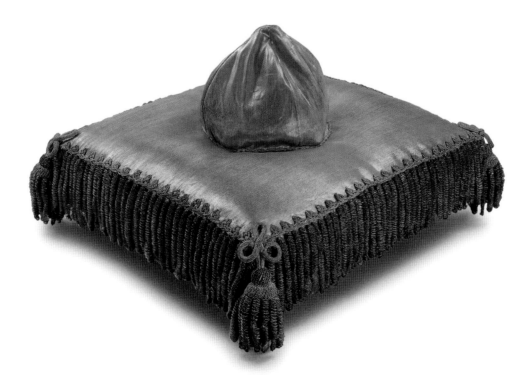

OFFICER'S UNIFORM OF THE PREOBRAZHENSKY LIFE GUARDS REGIMENT BELONGING TO EMPEROR PAUL I, 1796

Saint Petersburg

ТК-3018, ТК-3019, ТК-1939, ТК-1552, ТК-212/1-2, ТК-1907/1-2

THE coronation of Paul I took place on 5 April 1797. On 2 May the Armoury was given 'His Imperial Majesty's dress'– an officer's uniform of the Preobrazhensky Life Guards Regiment. This regiment was the first of the two oldest Imperial Guards infantry regiments and the Emperor himself was its patron.

This uniform is made of green wool with red velvet edging on the collar and has a fastening, which could be modified depending on the season. The silver stars with gold and enamel sewn to the front of the coat belong to the Order of Saint Andrew and the Order of Saint Alexander Nevsky. The white gloves were designed with gauntlets that covered the cuffs of the uniform coat. The back of the white wool waistcoat could be tightened by lacing and was worn tucked into the pantaloons, where it was fastened by means of two large hooks. The trousers were worn inside the patent leather boots, which had steel spurs. The black felt bicorn was trimmed with white plumes. From 1746 these feathers were the privilege of officers and generals of the Guard.

It is generally believed that this was the uniform worn

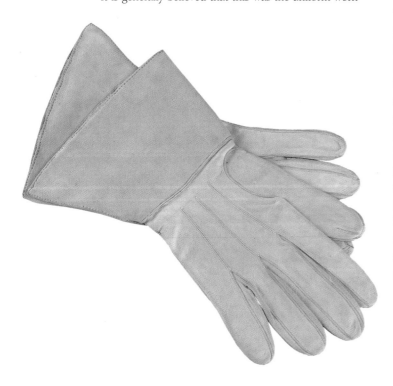

by Paul I for his coronation. However, ink inscriptions on the boots and the lining of the coat indicate that they were made approximately a year prior to that occasion and that he wore them nine months before his coronation. A similar uniform is kept at the State Museum-Preserve Pavlovsk, the Emperor's former residence near Saint Petersburg. The inscription '[Paul I] was crowned in this uniform. He was pleased to wear it on 5 April 1797 at the Kremlin Palace in Moscow' suggests that the uniform given to the Armoury was one of the sample 'Gatchina uniforms', which the future Emperor designed for the army he began creating at his Gatchina residence in 1782.[8]

The day after his accession, Paul I ordered all Guards regiments to adopt the style of military uniform that he had chosen for his coronation dress. The introduction of a strictly regulated military uniform was the start of a campaign against the permissive atmosphere that had prevailed in the Guards regiments. During the last decade of the reign of Catherine the Great, officers had their uniforms made 'according to personal taste, short and with high collars' and 'a particular model of elegance was the round hat *à l'anglaise* [in English style], which they wore almost all the time.'[9] In France during the era of the Directory (1794–9), the English round hat and coat with tails had come to epitomize free-thinking and revolutionary spirit and had similar connotations in the Russian capital where they had become popular. This style of Anglo-French dress did not appeal to Paul, who held extremely negative views about the French Revolution; he declared war against such fashions and promoted Prussian-style military uniform because it exemplified State order. The cut of this coat evoked a previous French model that epitomized the values of the *ancien régime*. The fact that Paul chose to introduce this style of uniform to the Russian Army and to wear it for his coronation was a conscious political decision and a clear demonstration of his adherence to the solid beginnings of the monarchy.

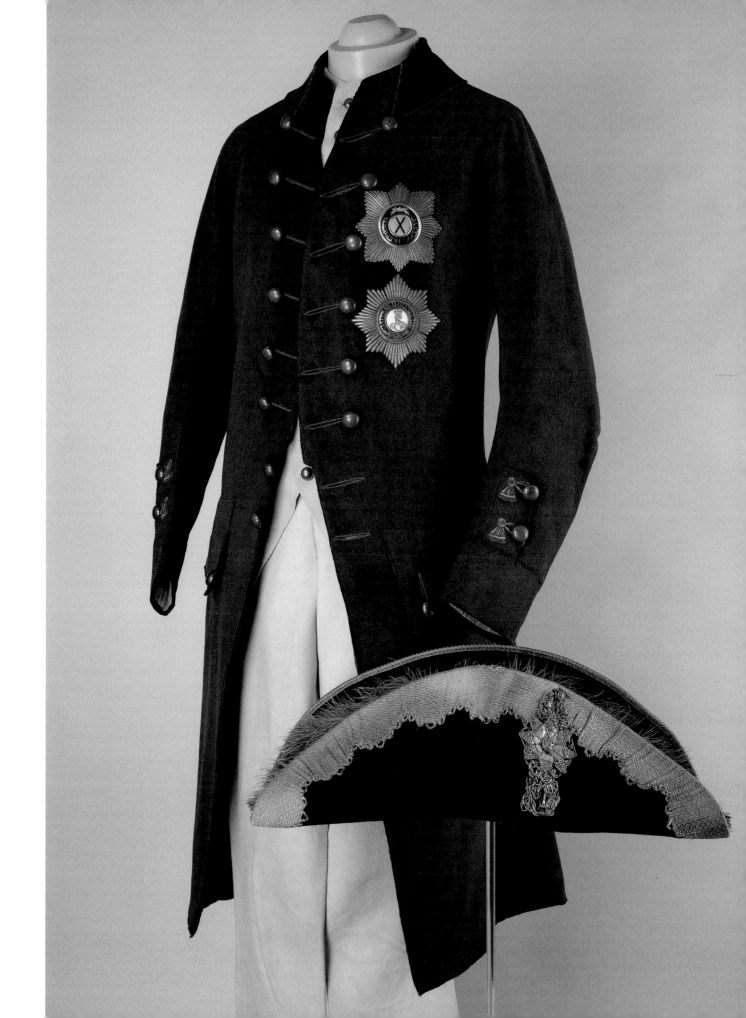

CORONATION HERALD'S LIVERY, 18TH CENTURY

Russia

TK-1616, TK-1618, TK-1604, TK-1557, TK-1399/1-2

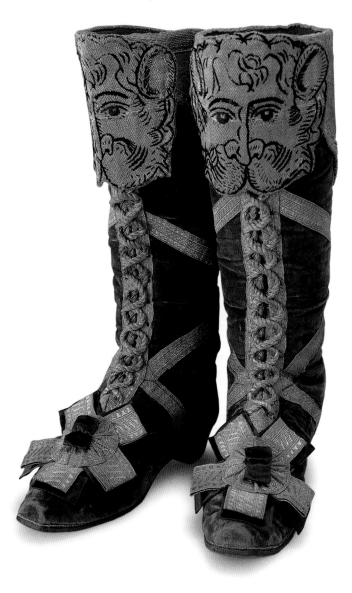

IN the first quarter of the eighteenth century, the Emperor created a body of heralds to serve the Imperial Court. At the West European courts the role of the herald involved a number of diplomatic duties, including the expert organization of coronation celebrations and other court festivities, where the heralds also took on the role of master of ceremonies. The key component of his livery was the tabard whose front and back were decorated with the coat of arms of the sovereign they represented. From 1724, two heralds participated in coronation festivities in Russia. First, they went round Moscow reading out the proclamation of the coronation. Subsequently, they led the coronation procession and stood as Guards of Honour at the Imperial throne. Although symbolic, the colour of the heralds' livery did change during the Imperial period. For the coronation of Emperor Paul I they were made from green and red velvet. The State Emblem of the Russian Empire was embroidered on the front and back of the tabard (*dalmatik*) in ochre-coloured silk. Three plumes of feathers were attached to their hats, which were trimmed in gold braid. The livery also included a pair of gloves and a white satin scarf with a gold fringe.[10]

Particularly decorative are the velvet boots with red leather heels. The tops of the boots feature ornamented flaps that are designed to resemble wings and 'masks' in the form of lions' heads, embroidered in silk on a gilt ground. The colour and decorative features of the boots suggest that they may have been modelled on patricians' boots of the late Roman Empire – the *calcei patricii*, which were bound to the calves with leather thongs and decorated with images of lions' heads. Winged lions featured on the knee caps of knights' armour in the Middle Ages, and participants in knights' carousels in the seventeenth and eighteenth centuries used similar images to decorate the tops of their boots.

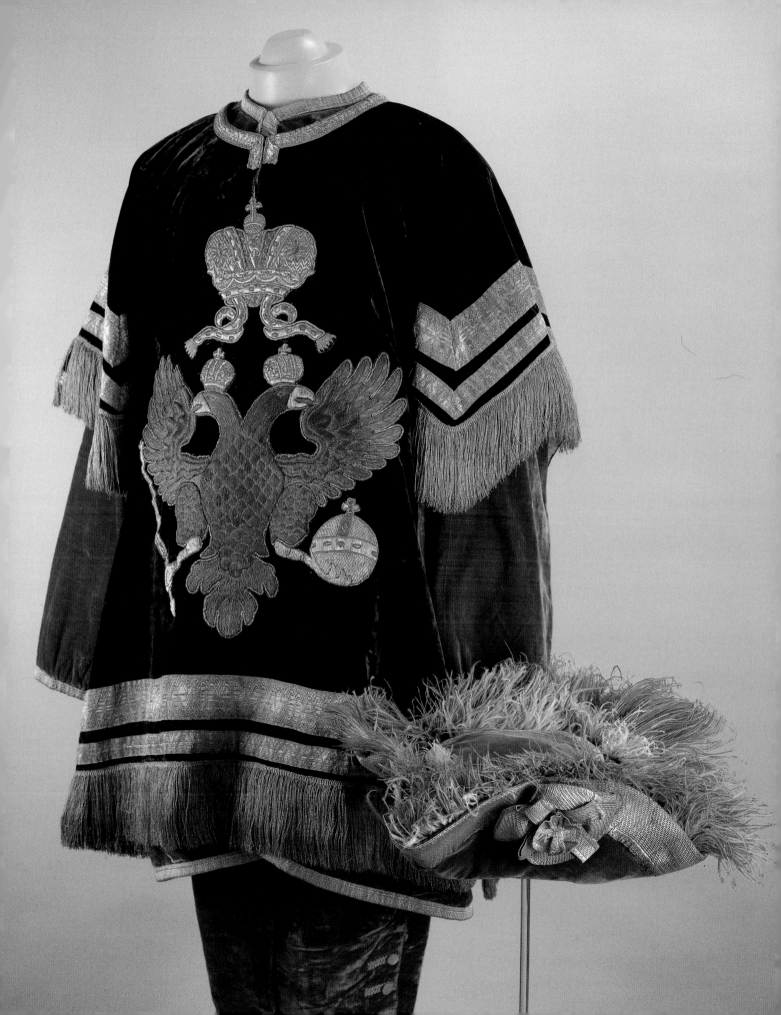

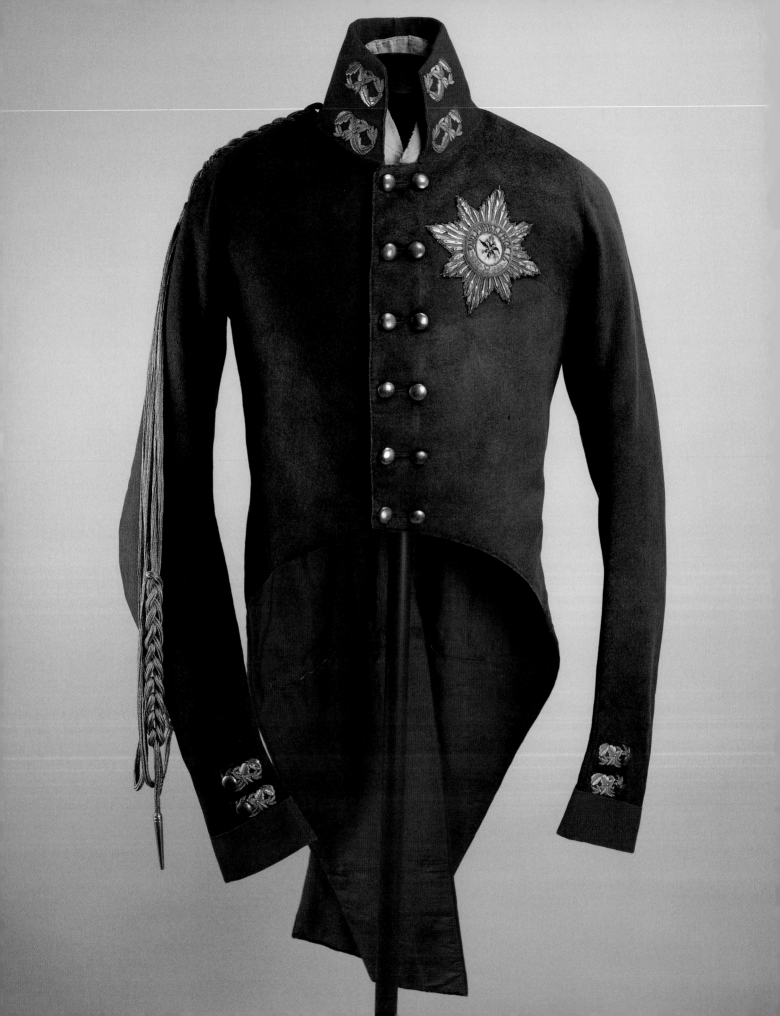

CORONATION COAT OF EMPEROR ALEXANDER I, 1801

Moscow
ТК-3020

FOLLOWING his father's example, Emperor Alexander I chose to wear the officer's uniform of the Preobrazhensky Life Guards Regiment for his coronation on 15 September 1801. In his coronation portrait he wears full dress uniform, an ermine mantle and the chain and star of the Order of Saint Andrew. The throne stands to his right, alongside a table bearing the crown and orb. In a recess to the left is a sculpture of Catherine the Great, who always saw her grandson as her heir and successor.

The short coat with long tails is made of green wool and has a high standing collar made of red wool and embroidered in gold with intertwined oak and laurel branches.[11] The star of the Order of Saint Andrew is sewn to the front of the coat; the points of the star are worked in silver foil and the centre is embroidered. On the right shoulder is an aiguillette of gold cord. The ensemble also includes a white wool waistcoat, white chamois leather trousers, patent leather boots and spurs, and a black felt hat with a plume of ostrich feathers. There is an inscription inside the left sleeve of the coat testifying to the fact that it was made in September 1801 in Moscow by Count Alexander Nikolaevich Golitsyn, one of the Emperor's confidants.[12]

It is known that Alexander was personally involved in creating a new uniform for the Russian army, and after his accession he showed a keen interest in matters relating to army attire. Having fallen behind in the European military fashion stakes as a result of Paul I's conservatism, Russia immediately began to make up for lost time and her army was soon considered one of the smartest in Europe after the British army. The British army had already adopted this style of uniform in 1797, but in Russia, prior to Alexander's coronation, changes had been made only to the uniforms of the Artillery units and Generals. The officers of the Preobrazhensky Life Guards Regiment received their new uniforms in 1802; thus, Alexander's coronation uniform is an experimental model. According to eyewitness accounts,

the Tsar's court came to resemble a soldiers' barracks. The Emperor's office was full of orderlies, messengers and lance-corporals modelling the uniforms of various troops, and the Emperor would spend hours with them, making chalk marks on their coats and undergarments amidst samples of moustache brushes, boot brushes, button-polishing sticks and other similar sundries.[13]

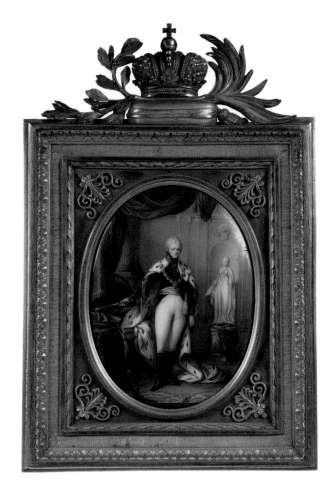

D.I. Evreinov, Portrait of Emperor Alexander I.
Saint Petersburg – miniature; mounting – bronze workshop of P. Azhi. 1802–1804.
MP-9065.

CORONATION HERALD'S TABARD, 1826

Russia

TK-1597

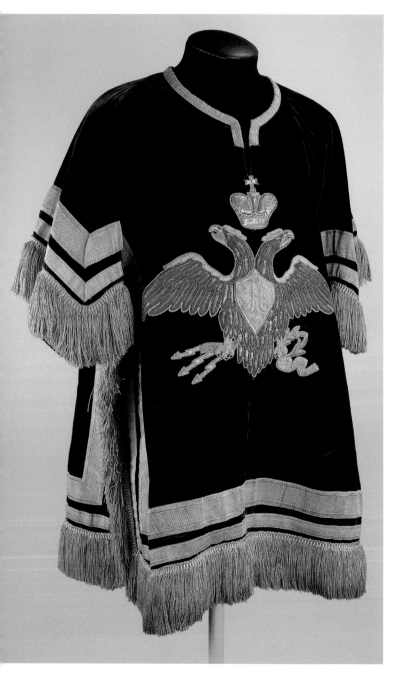

THIS tabard of green velvet, trimmed with gold braid and a thick, luxurious fringe, was made for the coronation of Emperor Nicholas I. Its luxurious materials are an illustration of the substantial sums spent on the costumes of coronation heralds, and the enormous significance attached to their role. The Russian Emblem with the Emperor's monogram is embroidered with coloured silk, gold thread and sequins on the front and back. This version of the State Emblem, named 'the eagle with spread wings', was first introduced during the reign of Emperor Alexander I, while the laurel wreath and thunderbolt in the talons of the eagle had appeared even earlier, featuring on the badges of the Order of Saint Andrew in February 1800 during the reign of Emperor Paul I. The use of military attributes such as swords, laurel wreaths, torches with flames at both ends, and double thunderbolts with arrows and ribbons undoubtedly reflected the long, hard battles that Russia fought at the end of the eighteenth and beginning of the nineteenth centuries, the patriotic fervour that victory encouraged, and the international recognition that Russia received as a result of her military triumphs. Particularly significant in this context were the defeat of Napoleon's invasion in 1812 and the foreign military campaigns of 1813–14.

COAT FROM THE CORONATION ENSEMBLE OF EMPEROR NICHOLAS I, 1826

Russia
TK-3022

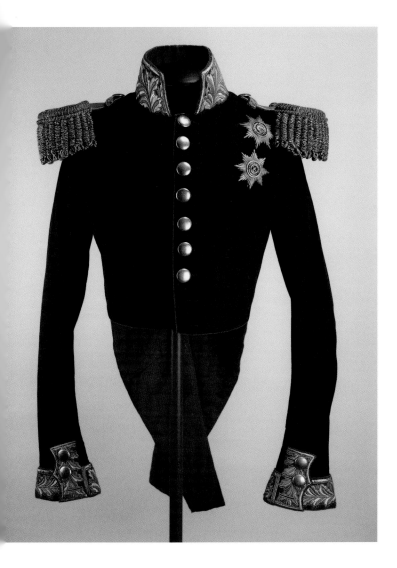

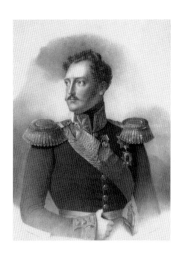

Portrait of Emperor
Nicholas I, first half of
1830s, Lithograph by
F. Jentzen, from a portrait
by F. Krüger.
*Inscription: Königl[ich] Lith.
Institut zu Berlin (on the front,
in the bottom right-hand corner),
N.d.N gem. V. F.Krüger lith.
V. Jentzen (in the left-hand
corner). GR-4773/1-2.*

For his coronation, which took place on 22 August 1826, Nicholas chose a general's coat with gold embroidery in the form of a garland of oak leaves. It had been adopted by the Russian army in January 1808. There are gold epaulettes on the shoulders and stars of the Orders of Saint Andrew and Saint Vladimir on the front. The coat is made of dark-green wool, and the collar, the lining of the tails, the piping and the French-style cuffs are red. This cuff type replaced Prussian-style cuffs in December 1802 at the beginning of the reign of Alexander I. A historical anecdote tells how, on one of his inspections, an officer of his retinue noticed that the Emperor had forgotten to do up the bottom buttons of his cuffs and pointed out to him that his cuffs were not buttoned up according to regulations. 'Everything the Emperor does is done according to regulations', answered Alexander, and from that moment the fashion for leaving the lower buttons of the cuffs undone became widespread amongst officers throughout the army, so that over time buttonholes were no longer even cut.[14]

Nicholas's coronation uniform included a striped silver sash with large tassels and a sword-knot, long narrow trousers of white wool, white elkskin gloves, patent leather boots with steel spurs, and a black felt hat with a plume of white, black and yellow feathers.

TO emphasize the legitimacy and dynastic continuity of his succession, Emperor Nicholas I chose to attend his coronation wearing the military uniform of the preceding reign. He had abandoned civilian attire completely in 1814 in favour of military uniform, which carried unquestionable authority in society as a symbol of valour after Napoleon's defeat in Russia in 1812.

CORONATION UNIFORM OF EMPEROR ALEXANDER II, 1856

Russia

HELMET – SAINT PETERSBURG, COURT MANUFACTURER OF OFFICERS' ACCOUTREMENTS E.D. BITNER [15]

TK-1988, TK-1917, TK-1918, TK-1558, TK-1904/1-2

THREE months after his accession Emperor Alexander II introduced a series of reforms, one of which concerned the cut of the Guards' uniforms. The characteristic decorative elements remained the same, but the coat changed to a double-breasted, thigh-length style. An official publication explained that the reform was carried out in the interests of simplification and comfort. An old Russian name, *polukaftan* (short coat), was given to the new type of jacket, thus linking it to traditional national men's dress and indicating that the reform was part of the much wider policy of official nationalism, an appeal to the nation's patriotic sentiment.

Alexander wore the new general's uniform for his coronation. The dark-green wool coat with red collar and cuffs is fastened with gilt buttons decorated with the State Emblem and has gilt embroidery around the collar, the cuffs and the pocket flaps. A silver sash woven with black and orange was worn round the waist. Insignia of the Orders of Saint Andrew and Saint Vladimir are pinned to the front

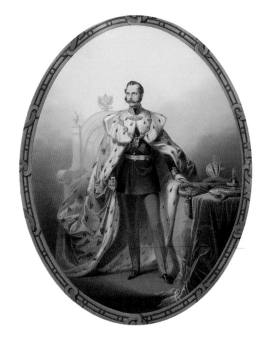

Portrait of Emperor Alexander II. Chromolithograph by Walter.
From the book 'Opisanie svyashchennogo koronovaniya ikh imperatorskikh velichestv gosudarya imperatora Aleksandra II i imperatritsy Marii Aleksandrovny vseya Rossii'. (1856), Moscow Kremlin Museums.

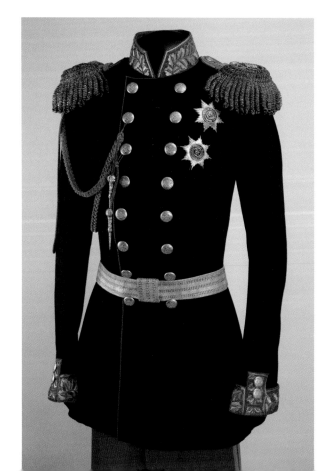

of the tunic. The epaulettes are made of the thick spiral fringe reserved for generals and decorated with the monogram of Emperor Nicholas I. The monogram and the aiguillette were signs used to distinguish members of the Imperial retinue and they were given to Alexander to mark his coming of age (17 April 1834) when he was Grand Duke. He also received the title of aide-de-camp. The heir to the throne considered this appointment to be a great honour and kept these badges of distinction on his coat when he acceded to the throne.

Alexander's coronation uniform has scarlet wool trousers with gold braid stripes down the side seam and leather stirrups that were worn over the boots to keep the trousers in place. A black leather helmet with a bronze gilt decoration and a plume of cock feathers, black patent leather boots with silver-plated copper spurs, and white kidskin gloves completed the outfit.

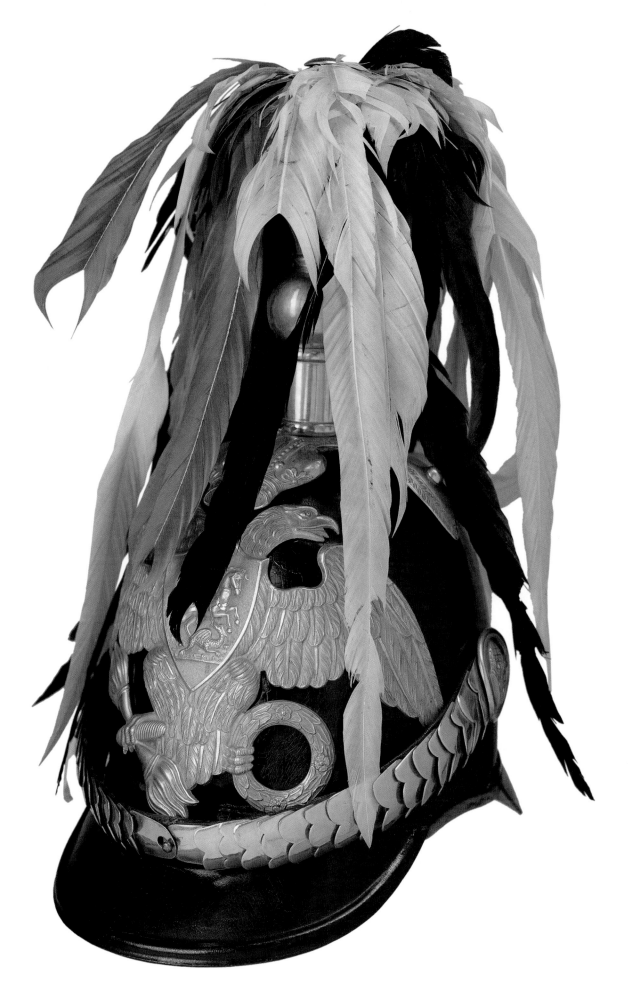

CORONATION COAT OF EMPEROR ALEXANDER III, 1883

Saint Petersburg
TAILOR — F. RAUSER
TK-3039

EMPEROR Alexander III believed that a truly Russian person should dress simply and be unaffected in manners and speech. In this respect, he served as a role model for his subjects. To receive his ministers, he 'usually dressed very simply and only in military uniform, which was already quite

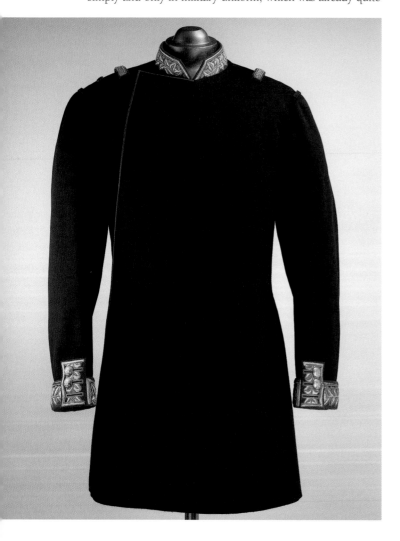

worn.'[16] When attending receptions and balls, and even for his coronation ceremony on 15 May 1883, he also chose uniform, as depicted in the official record of that event, *The Holy Coronation of His Majesty Emperor Alexander III.*[17] His choice did not detract from his authority, for, according to the finance minister S.Yu. Witte, 'even if we hadn't known that he was the Emperor, he could have entered the room wearing whatever he liked and would still have made an impression.'[18]

It was Alexander III's wish that the uniform of the Russian army should be designed to resemble Russian national costume as closely as possible. The only item from Alexander's coronation uniform that was handed over to the Armoury after the ceremony was his full dress general's coat, from which the epaulettes and Insignia of the Orders had already been removed. The coat is made of dark-green wool and has a standing collar and red cuffs and edging; it is cut following the lines of a *zipun*, or folk coat, wrapping to one side. The buttons that fasten it are concealed under the lapel. Although this new style of uniform was undeniably practical, it was criticized for its gloomy simplicity and crude cut.

F. Rauser, tailor to His Imperial Majesty, made this coat.[19] The vertical slit in the front of the coat at chest level was specifically for the coronation ceremony so that the Emperor could be anointed with oil on his chest. Grand Duke Konstantin Romanov noted in his diary that in a conversation with Emperor Nicholas II on the eve of his coronation the Emperor 'recalled how difficult it was … to convince the late Sovereign that there should be a slit in the front of the coat for the ceremony of Holy Unction.'[20] This modification was apparently necessary due to the cut of the coat and had not been necessary before in Russia. It was, however, a feature of the coronation garments of the French Kings Louis XV and Louis XVI.

CORONATION COAT OF EMPEROR NICHOLAS II, 1896

Saint Petersburg
TAILOR — N.I. NORDENSTREM
ACCOUTREMENTS SUPPLIER — M.I. SKOSYREV
TK-3040

EMPEROR Nicholas II 'considered himself a soldier, the first professional soldier of his Empire.'[21] He appeared before his subjects at his coronation on 14 May 1896 wearing a colonel's uniform of the Preobrazhensky Life Guards Regiment. Like his grandfather and great-grandfather before him, he saw the Guards as a kind of extended family. Having undertaken his military service in the Preobrazhensky Regiment before his accession and achieved the rank of colonel, he preferred its uniform above all others. He chose to retain this rank when he was Emperor, taking pride in the fact that he was 'still just a colonel.'[22] On visiting Nicholas at Tsarskoe Selo on 7 December 1895, Grand Duke Konstantin Romanov noted in his diary: 'I asked the Tsar which uniform he intended to wear for his coronation. He said that he would wear ours, the Preobrazhensky uniform.'[23]

Nicholas's uniform is made from dark-green wool with white edging. This detail was accorded to the First Infantry Division of the regiment in memory of victory at the Battle of Gangut in 1714. The coat has a red collar and cuffs, skilfully embroidered in gilt thread. Its epaulettes bear the monogram of Alexander III. According to eyewitness accounts during the coronation ceremony the sovereign himself moved aside the small square folding flap, specially made on the breast of his coat, so that he could be annointed.[24]

The entire uniform of Nicholas II was ordered from N.I. Nordenstrem, the famous 'king of Russian military tailors, who had dressed the best of the Guards' dandies.'[25] Nordenstrem was 'a true artist in his work,' and the uniforms tailored by him 'bore the hallmark of strict elegance and good taste.'[26] The aiguillettes, epaulettes and buttons for Nicholas' coats were ordered from the supplier of officers' accoutrements M.I. Skosyrev, who from 1860 was 'privileged to supply accoutrements for the personal wardrobe of His Majesty.'[27]

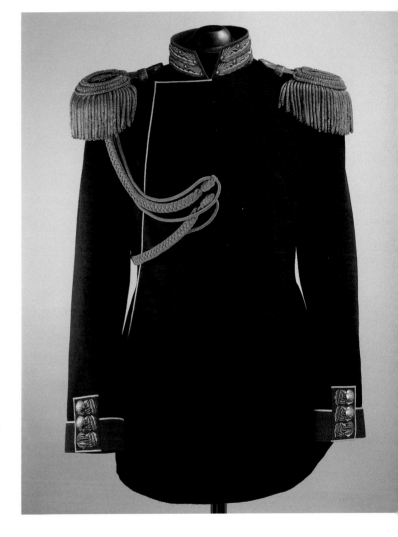

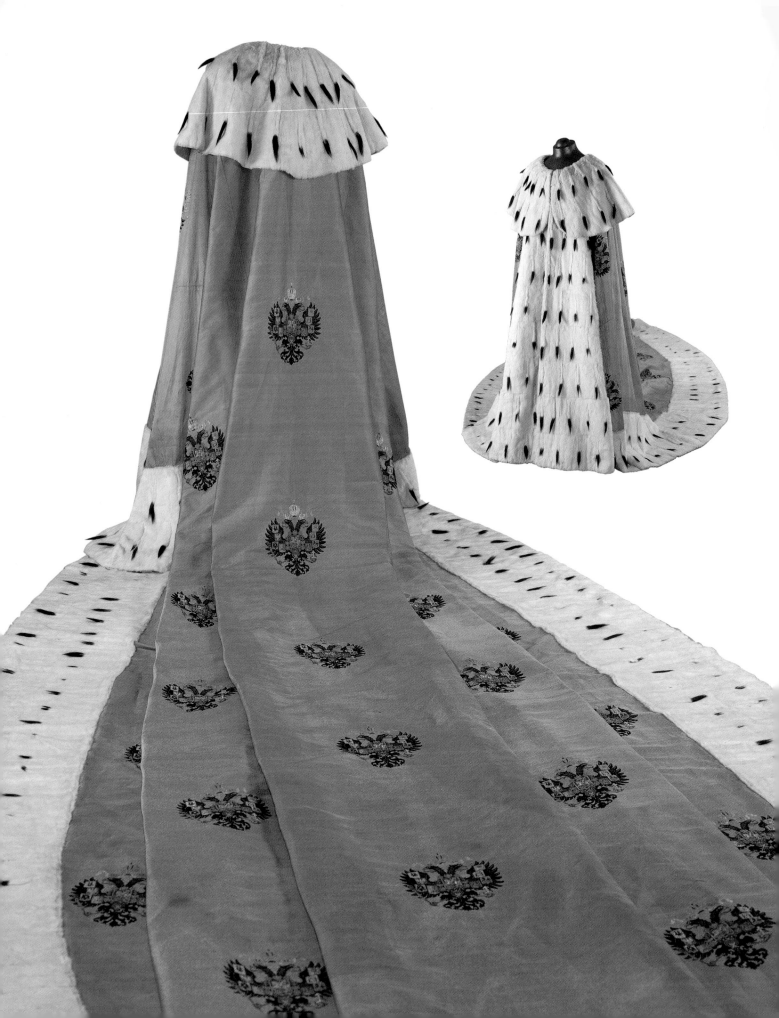

CORONATION MANTLE, 1896

Moscow, Saint Petersburg

SILK — A. & V. SAPOZHNIKOVY; ERMINE — PAVEL SOROKOUMOVSKY AND SONS
MANTLE-MAKER — MADAME OLGA
DESIGN OF THE MANTLE AND STATE EMBLEM — ACADEMICIAN A. TROMBITSKY[28]
TK-2601

THE mantle became a part of the Russian Imperial Regalia
in 1724. A new mantle was made for every coronation in
the same style until the last Russian Imperial coronation.
Three identical mantles were made for Emperor Nicholas II,
for Empress Alexandra Feodorovna and for the Dowager
Empress Maria Feodorovna, who also took part in the
ceremony. These mantles differed from those made for
previous coronations: instead of the State Emblem being
embroidered onto plain cloth of gold, eagles were woven
into a fabric made by Sapozhnikovy.[29]

These luxurious mantles were all 7m (23ft) long and
weighed approximately 13kg (28lb). They were made in the
famous Saint Petersburg workshop of Madame Olga who was
the 'official supplier to the Court of Her Imperial Majesty',
making 'Dresses, mantillas and court trains'.[30] Gold buckles
with cut emeralds, previously used to decorate the coronation
mantles of Alexander II and Alexander III, were brought from
the Armoury to be sewn onto the Emperor's mantle. The
trimming and capes of the three mantles used 2,691 ermine
skins. A coronation rehearsal was held two days before the
ceremony, during which three pages, dressed in linen copies
of the mantles, gave instructions on how the trains were to be
carried and arranged during the ceremony. It took seven
chamberlains to carry the train of each mantle during the
procession.

After the coronation, the Emperor's mantle was used on
one more occasion – for the staging of the opening ceremony
of the first session of the State Council and State Duma, which
took place on 27 April 1906 in Saint George's Hall, the throne
room of the Winter Palace in Saint Petersburg.

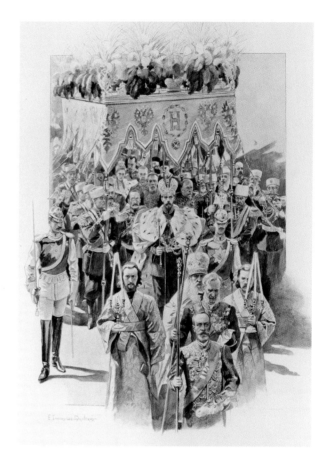

Ceremonial procession during the coronation of Emperor Nicholas II.
From a drawing by E. Samokish-Sudkovskaya. From the book 'Koronatsionnyi
sbornik' (Saint Petersburg, 1899).

CORONATION HERALD'S LIVERY, 1856, 1883, 1896

Moscow, Saint Petersburg

SILK — A. & V. SAPOZHNIKOVY[31]
EMBROIDERY ON THE TABARD — THE GOLD EMBROIDERY SHOP A. LOMAN[32]
BOOTS — E. SHTUMPF;[33] EMBROIDERY ON THE BOOTS — THE GOLD EMBROIDERY SHOP M. ZALEMAN[34]
HAT — FABRIQUE DE CHAPEAUX BRUNO FRÈRES[35]
GLOVES — MORISSON ALPHONSE BERNY SUCCESSEUR GANTIER DE PARIS[36]
TK-1624, TK-1630, TK-1631, TK-1225, TK-1584, TK-241/1-2, TK-1632/1-2, MP-9170

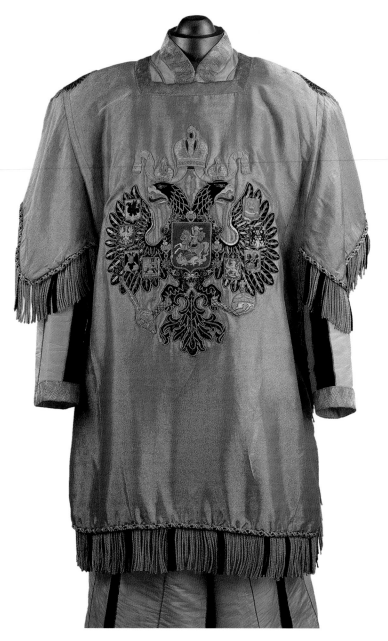

DURING preparation for the coronation of Emperor Alexander II, the Master Herald Baron V.B. Kyone proposed a design of a coronation herald's livery based on the heraldic colours of the Empire: gold (yellow), silver (white) and black. The Emperor approved the sketch, and the same design was used for the next two coronations. This uniform comprises several items: the tabard, hat and gloves were made for Alexander III's coronation, and the quilted coat, trousers, boots and sash were made for Nicholas II's. The ensemble is completed by a sword on a gold cross-belt and a gilded silver staff, topped with an enamelled double-headed eagle. This staff was originally made for Alexander II's coronation and was then used for subsequent coronations.

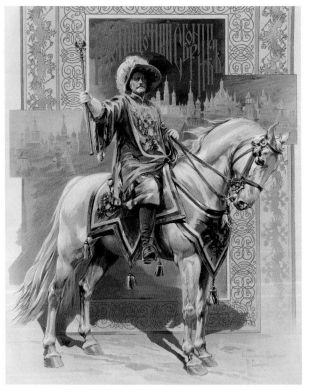

Herald at the coronation of Emperor Nicholas II.
Engraving. From the book 'Koronatsionnyi sbornik'
(Saint Petersburg, 1899).

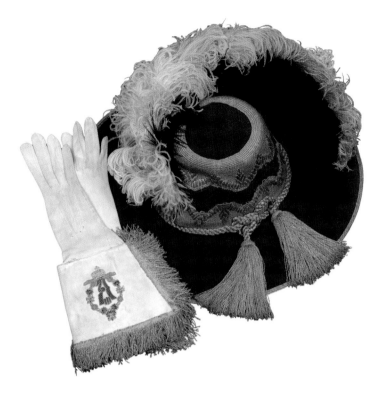

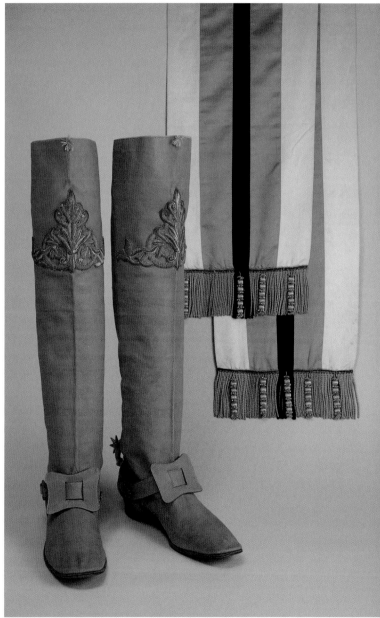

The tabard is made from cloth of gold bought in Moscow from A&V Sapozhnikovy, one of the leading Russian textile manufacturing firms in the second half of the nineteenth century and at the beginning of the twentieth century. It was renowned worldwide for the excellent quality of its heavy patterned silks. The front, back and shoulders of the tabard feature Lesser State Emblems, which were embroidered in accordance with a new design, created by the artist A.A. Fadeev and approved by the Emperor.[37]

The tabard was worn over a coat, made from silk satin and moiré and decorated with gilt braid, and three-coloured wide breeches. They were made by K. Pipar, wardrobe master of the Management of Imperial Theatres. As accessories, the herald wore a musketeer-style red velvet hat with ostrich feathers, gold braid and tassels, white kidskin gloves bearing the monogram of Alexander III and embroidered boots with gold spurs. These were made according to the design of E.P. Ponomarev, artist to the Imperial Theatres.[38] The addition of a three-coloured satin sash with a gold fringe distinguished members of the ceremonial detachment that accompanied the heralds as they read the Imperial proclamation of the coronation throughout Moscow.

PHELONION, 1896

Moscow
SILK — A. & V. SAPOZHNIKOVY
TK-161

AT Nicholas II's coronation, the clergymen of the Moscow
Kremlin wore vestments that had been specially made for
the occasion using magnificent brocade from the famous
Russian textile manufactory A. & V. Sapozhnikovy, suppliers
of fabric to the Imperial Court since 1852. This phelonion
was made for the priest performing the church ceremony in
the Cathedral of the Assumption. It is one of the principal
liturgical vestments of the Orthodox priest and symbolizes
the crucifixtion of Christ.

The main element of the pattern is the image of a
double-headed eagle beneath a crown, holding a sceptre in
its right claw. The design was modelled on a Venetian golden
velvet with eagles that was imported for the Moscow court
in the second half of the seventeenth century, and used to
make a ceremonial coat for Tsar Feodor Alexeevich, the elder
brother of the future Emperor Peter I. In 1696 this coat
was remade into a vestment for the patriarch (the head of
Russian Church) and is kept in the Armoury collection to
this day.

In creating the fabric for the coronation celebrations of
1896, Russian weavers successfully reproduced the pattern
of the Italian velvet on brocade using a different technique,
recreating the effect of the ancient raised velvet using silver
gilt threads of varying shades and thickness.

Each part of the phelonion has its own symbolic
significance. The shoulders are meant to suggest traces of
flogging on the shoulders of Christ and are traditionally
made from a different coloured fabric. The shoulders of this
phelonion are made from gilt brocade of the same colour
as the main body, but in a different texture and design.
Motifs of branches and leaves are woven on the front of the
phelonion using loops of gilt thread on a plain background,
and there is an image of a radiating crown on the back.

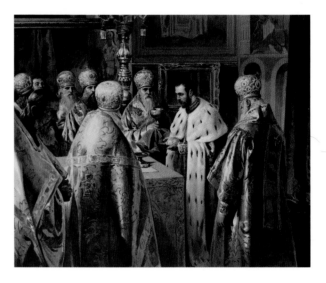

Holy Communion of His Imperial Majesty Sovereign
Emperor Nikolai Alexandrovich.
From a watercolour by K. Lebedev. From the book 'Koronatsionnyi sbornik'
(Saint Petersburg, 1899).

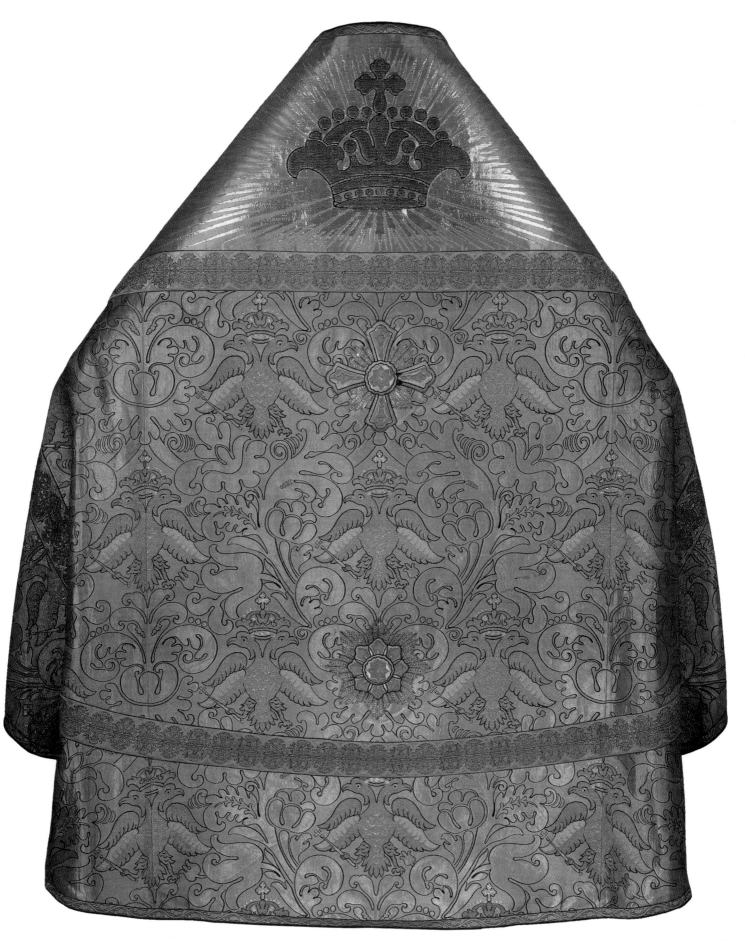

45

PART OF CORONATION CANOPY, 1896

Moscow

EMBROIDERY — ASCENSION CONVENT

TK-3349/1

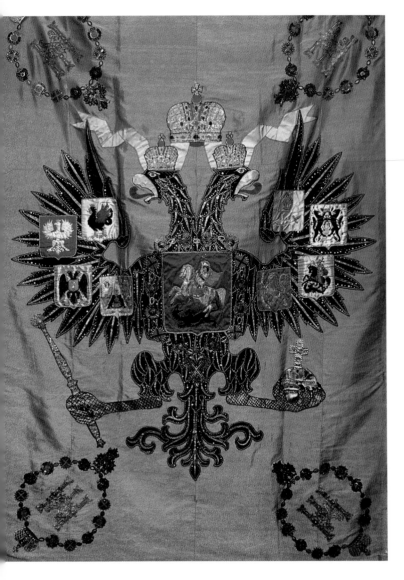

AN enormous canopy was usually carried in the coronation procession, which left the Kremlin Palace and made its way to the Cathedral of the Assumption on the other side of Cathedral Square (see also p.2). This canopy consisted of two layers of fabric stretched over a rectangular frame, the lower layer being decorated with the State Emblem of the Russian Empire. The canopy was framed with four horizontal panels hanging down from around the top and a gilded metal cornice. It was topped with bunches of ostrich feathers, and carried on gilded silver poles, held during the procession by the aide-de-camp generals in velvet slings (see p.41). If a single monarch was being crowned, eight poles were used to support the canopy; for the Emperor and Empress, it was twice as big and was carried on 16 poles. When the Dowager Empress took part in the coronation, a separate canopy was made for her.

This fabric is part of the canopy made for the Dowager Empress Maria Feodorovna for the coronation of Emperor Nicholas II. The centre is decorated with the Lesser State Emblem of the Russian Empire (approved in 1883). The monogram of the Dowager Empress appears in each of the corners, surrounded by chains of the Order of Saint Andrew. The appliqué work is composed of satin, velvet, cloth of gold and gold foil, and the embroidery uses metal and silk thread and sequins. For the coronation of 1896, all the gold embroidery for the State Emblems and the monograms of Their Imperial Majesties were produced in Moscow's Orthodox convents, which were renowned for their superior skill in this specialized art. Under the supervision of the Mother Superior Eugenia, eight nuns from Moscow's Ascension Convent, a female cloister within the Kremlin's Cathedral of the Ascension, embroidered this canopy.[39]

CUSHION FOR THE THRONE OF EMPEROR NICHOLAS II, 1896

Moscow
EMBROIDERY – ASCENSION CONVENT
TK-1308

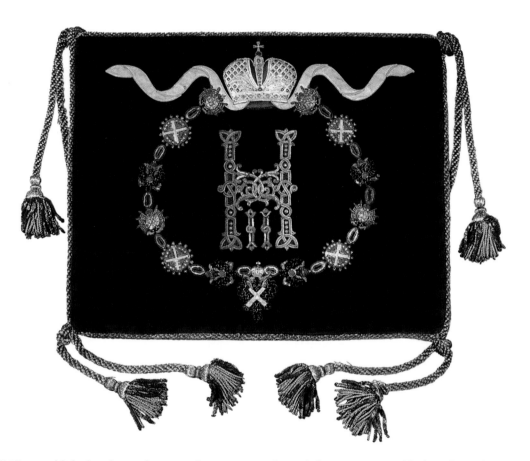

ACCORDING to established tradition, the Imperial coronation ceremony used ancient royal thrones, which are kept in the Armoury collection to this day. These thrones were carried from the Treasury to the Cathedral of the Assumption, where they were placed under a canopy on a specially built dais. For the coronation of Nicholas II in 1896, the so-called 'ivory' throne belonging to Ivan the Terrible (ruled 1547–84) was used for Empress Alexandra Feodorovna, the 'diamond' throne belonging to Tsar Alexey Mikhailovich Romanov (ruled 1645–76) was used for the Dowager Empress Maria Feodorovna, and the 'golden'

throne belonging to Tsar Mikhail Feodorovich Romanov (reigned 1613–45) was used for the Emperor himself. Cushions of red velvet were attached to the seats and backs of the thrones with gold tasselled cords.

This cushion, decorated with a monogram beneath an Imperial crown and surrounded by the chain of the Order of Saint Andrew, was made for the back of the throne used by Emperor Nicholas II. After the coronation ceremony, the thrones and their cushions were taken to the Kremlin Palace, where they were used by the Emperor, Empress and Dowager Empress during the celebratory dinner.

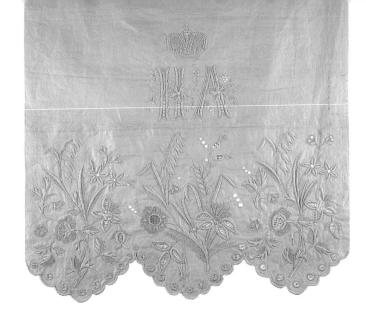

PRESENTATION CLOTHS, 1883, 1896

Poltava, Kharkov
TK-693, TK-711, TK-719

ONE of the most important rituals of the Imperial Court was the tradition of bringing bread and salt to the monarch after the coronation, and also during visits to various cities and establishments. This ancient folk custom was introduced into court ceremonials during the reign of Nicholas I. According to one contemporary commentator, it demonstrated 'the people's virtue and their gratitude to the Tsar, who does not stand aside from anyone and honours the customs of his forefathers.'[40]

Representatives of the nobility, the district councils, and the urban and rural populations of the Russian Empire attended the celebrations of the holy coronation in Moscow. They were invited to take part in the ceremonies and were permitted to express their congratulations to Their Imperial Majesties in the throne room of the Great Kremlin Palace, where special tables were set up for the purpose. The bread and salt were usually brought in on dishes specially made for the occasion, with salt-cellars made of silver, wood or porcelain. They were carried on cloths that had been embroidered by local craftsmen. As well as elements of folk embroidery, characteristic of the various provinces of the multinational Russian State, the decoration of these cloths usually featured the State Emblem of Imperial

Russia, the monograms of the Emperor and Empress and congratulations to the Imperial couple.

The white linen cloth decorated with cross stitch (which was traditionally used in Ukrainian embroidery), appliqué work and bobbin lace was a coronation gift to Emperor Alexander III from the nobility of Poltava Province (far right). Two inscriptions are embroidered on the cloth: 'To the Crowned Descendent of the Tsar, Chosen One of the Russian People and Tsar-Liberator' and 'To the Sovereign Successor, Reverential Good Wishes from the Nobility of Poltava.'

The second cloth (near right) is made of white silk and was given to Emperor Nicholas II by the nobility of the Kharkov Province. The State Emblem of the Russian Empire is embroidered at one end of the cloth, surrounded by the coats of arms of the district towns of Kharkov Province; at the other end, the coat of arms of Kharkov Province is surrounded by bouquets of wild flowers, sheaves of wheat, rakes and scythes, traditional symbols of peasant labour. The centre of the cloth features the monogram of the Emperor beneath a crown and also the Imperial Regalia arranged on their cushion.

The third cloth (above) was also made for the coronation of 1896, as indicated by the elegant combined monograms of Emperor Nicholas II and Empress Alexandra Feodorovna beneath a crown, embroidered in white on white. The pattern is made up of large bouquets of wheat and the Empress's favourite lilies-of-the-valley, which blossom in May, the month in which the coronation took place.

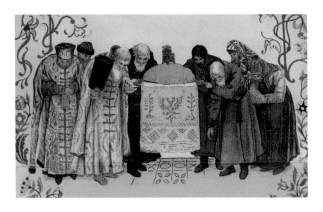

Ancient ceremony of bringing of bread and salt.
From a drawing by V.M. Vasnetsov. From the book Koronatsionnyi sbornik (Saint Petersburg, 1899).

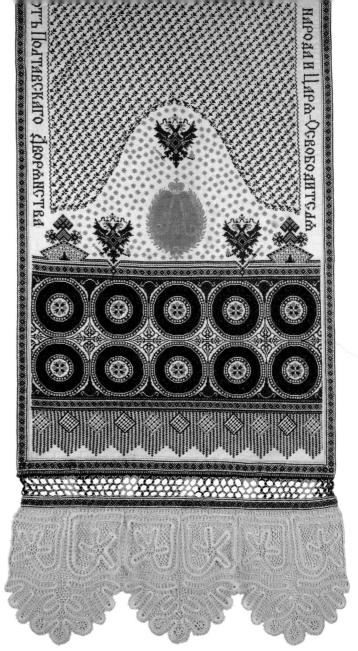

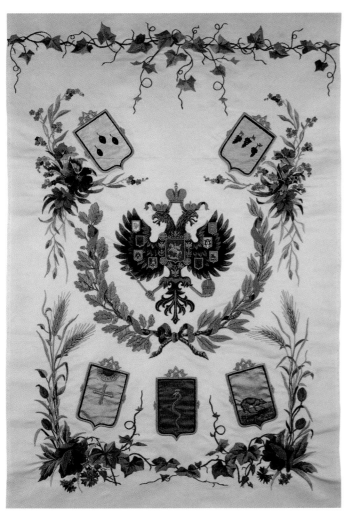

The Wardrobe of Emperor Peter II

'One cannot help but marvel at the vanity shown here in matters relating to dress: the local magnates wear a new outfit every holiday'.[1]

SO wrote the Spanish envoy to Russia in one of his reports, expressing his views on the customs that held sway in the court of Emperor Peter II. Unrestrained extravagance in the creation of new outfits characterized the first half of the eighteenth century, and in this respect the contents of the Emperor's own wardrobe are very revealing. After the sudden death of the young monarch in 1730, his entire wardrobe was kept for 36 years in the storerooms of the Kremlin Palace in Moscow before being sent to the Armoury in 1766 by command of Catherine the Great, with the exception of a few items that had been heavily damaged by moths. Pine chests and trunks, upholstered with seal fur and bound with iron, were sent to the Treasury. They contained 36 complete outfits including uniforms and hunting attire, 24 court dress coats, 21 waistcoats, 10 pairs of breeches, various items of outerwear, informal indoor wear, undergarments, 25 pairs of stockings, nine hats and 22 pairs of gloves. These clothes reveal that the young Peter was still growing, as his coronation suit is small in comparison with some other items.

All of these outfits and accessories are traditionally believed to have been ordered in France, although there is evidence to suggest that some of them were made in Russia. Documents have revealed the names of two craftsmen attached to the wardrobe of Peter II, both of whom were foreigners: the tailor Andris Appelgrimm and the Master of the Wardrobe Peter Bem. The latter would have been responsible not only for maintaining the wardrobe but also for advising on its contents.

Despite being nearly 300 years old, approximately half of the surviving items are still in almost perfect condition, which allows us to study in detail the design and cut of the Western European men's dress that had become a ubiquitous feature of court life by the time of Peter's accession to the throne in 1727. Developed in France under Louis XIV (reigned 1651–1715) and modified in the early eighteenth century, the dress of a gentleman featured a three-piece suit, consisting of a coat, waistcoat and breeches. It was made of silk (plain, brocade or velvet) or wool and decorated with metal lace or embroidery. The ensemble was usually complemented by a wig, a three-cornered hat, a linen cravat, lace ruffles, silk stockings and shoes with buckles.

The single-breasted, collarless coat was designed to fit snugly to the upper torso and to flare out from the waist. In order to create the fashionable shape, several side pleats were added, stiffened with gummed linen so that they flared out at the waist. A slit, held together by two pairs of buttons, was left in the side so that the wearer might access his sword, which he wore on a sword belt under the coat. The coat sleeves had large turn-back cuffs, which were often ornamented with trimmings or made of contrasting fabric. The coat was worn over a waistcoat with narrow sleeves, which was cut without side pleats, and the accompanying breeches had narrow legs but were voluminous round the hips.

The cut and decoration of clothes remained fairly consistent in Russia during the eighteenth century, although there are no fashion magazines to trace the changes. What changed was not the style but the patterns on the silk, as twice a year French designers created new patterns. The most expensive fabrics were woven using gilt and silver and silk thread and only the upper echelons of European society were able to afford such luxury. Their custom supported the main European silk-weaving houses where rather less elaborate silks were the mainstay of most businesses. As the composition of Peter's wardrobe corresponds precisely to the dates of his short reign

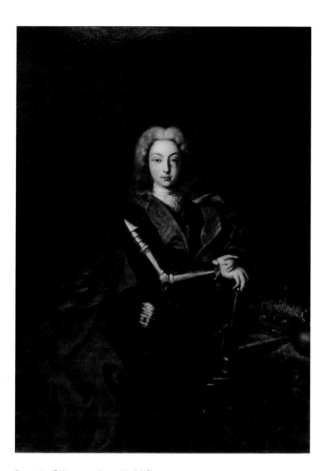

Portrait of Emperor Peter II, 18th century,
Russia, Zh-1948.

(7 May 1727–19 January 1730), it offers valuable insight into preferred styles in embroidery and on patterned silk fabrics during that period. The fabrics used for the dress of the Russian Emperor belong to a time when the emphasis was still on opulent grandeur.

By the second decade of the eighteenth century, baroque style had been superseded. The floral elements in the silk patterns gradually became more natural. The favourite motifs were semi-naturalistic flowers woven in polychrome silks, which were often combined in varying proportions with abstract ornamental motifs woven in silver and gilt thread. Garland-like patterns reminiscent of lace were also very fashionable at the time, but in the 1730s flowers had begun to dominate. All these characteristic elements of patterns at the end of the 1720s can be found in Peter's wardrobe, which shows that many of his clothes were made using the fashionable new silks of his day.

Unfortunately, no portrait survives of Peter in his fashionable court dress, though the artist Johan Paul Ludden, who arrived in Saint Petersburg from Brunswick in 1728, painted several portraits of the Emperor by order of the Russian court.

Peter's short reign was not distinguished by any State activity. Peter the Great had devoted scant attention to his grandson's upbringing and education, as he did not apparently entertain the possibility that he might one day take the throne. Following the death of Empress Catherine I, the 11-year-old orphan became a pawn in the hands of various court factions aspiring to rule the country, and Peter spent his short life in an atmosphere of court intrigues. He channelled his energies into his enjoyment of court entertainment and leisure pursuits, in which he was indulged by his advisers in their attempts to gain favour with the young Emperor and thus exert their influence on him. Count A.I. Osterman was particularly successful in this regard. Appointed as Peter's tutor, he drew up a timetable of studies for Peter, according to which 12 hours a week were to be allocated to the study of history, mathematics and geography. The remaining time was devoted to various games, dancing, riding, archery, music and the Tsar's favourite pastime – hunting. The heavily worn gaiters (see p.69), conserved in the Armoury, may well offer a tantalizing glimpse of his enthusiasm for such open-air activities.

COAT (*KAFTAN*) AND WAISTCOAT (*KAMZOL*), 1727–30

France
TK-2909, TK-2910

THIS lavish suit, consisting of coat and waistcoat, is the first item listed under formal attire in the inventory of Peter II's wardrobe. It was clearly made for a particularly important court ceremony, and its size, large in comparison with the majority of his other suits, indicates that it was probably for Peter's marriage, on the eve of which he died. The magnificent stateliness of the outfit is due to the combination of the colours crimson and gold. This colour combination was used in Russia in the seventeenth century for the Tsars' most formal attire. Raised metal lace, which was also an essential element of decoration of the formal outfits of the Tsars, is used in this ceremonial suit to harmonize garments made from two different fabrics of French manufacture.

The coat is made from cut and uncut velvet decorated with a small repeating pattern of flowers resembling carnations contained within ornamental compartments. Stylized flowers of a different kind, featuring leaves and buds on slender stems, are arranged between compartments. The lining is made from crimson silk. The skirts, large cuffs, pocket flaps and side slits of the coat are decorated with wide gilt lace with a heavy ornamental floral and foliate design. Close inspection reveals that the original lace trimming was clearly made to fit garments for an adult male. As Peter was still young and relatively small, the tailor seems to have folded the excess lace on the pocket flaps over and stitched the layers together along the sides of the skirts. The worked buttons have a purely decorative function, as there are no corresponding buttonholes. A braid loop and button are sewn onto the right shoulder for the purpose of attaching the sash of a chivalric order.

The waistcoat and the cuffs of the coat are made from patterned silk in a complex weave, consisting of a large-scale fanciful pattern of flowers, foliage and lace garlands. It incorporates both plain and twisted gilt thread to create a sparkling effect on the crimson ground. The waistcoat is decorated with gilt lace, which is narrower than that on the coat and of a slightly different pattern, and numerous buttons, of which only five actually fasten – four at the waist and one on the collar.

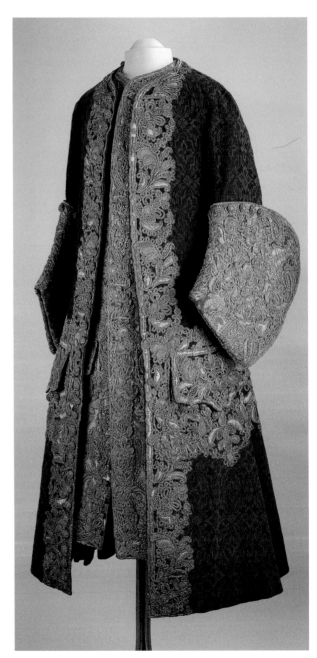

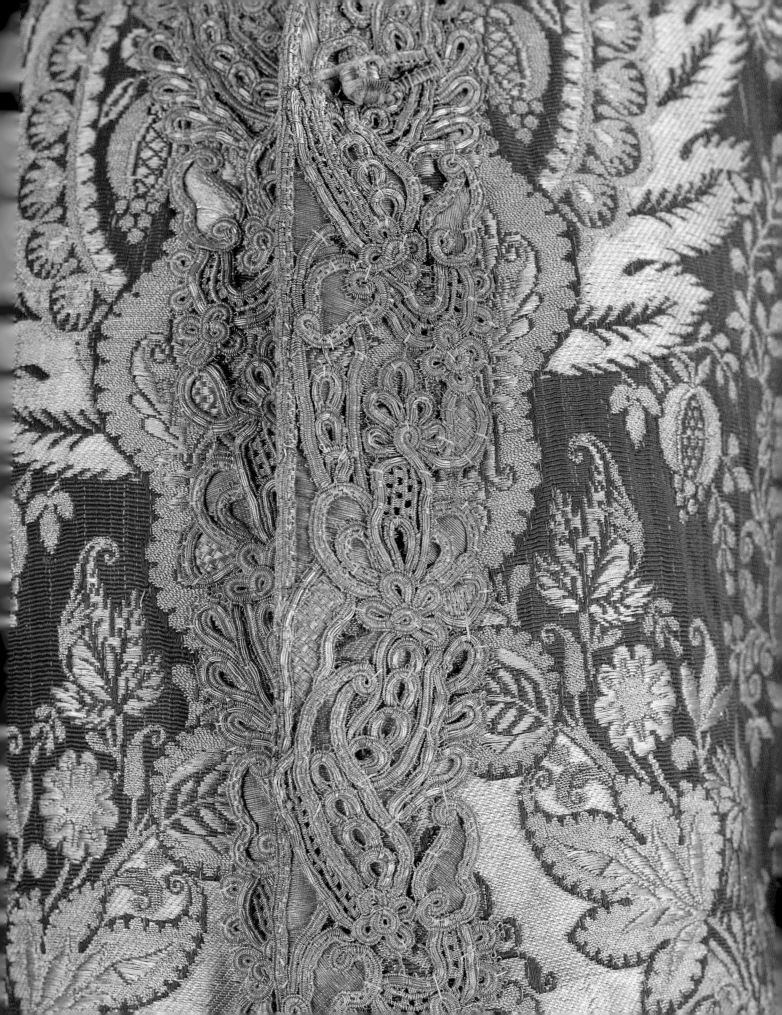

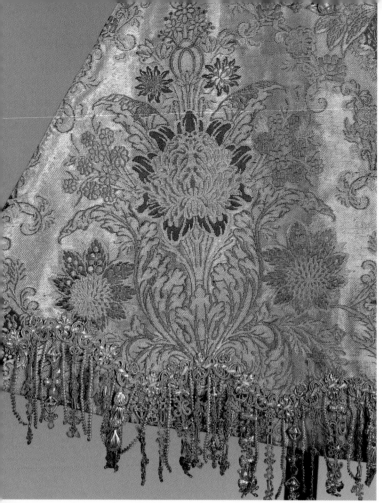

PETER'S wardrobe includes two formal outfits made of luxurious patterned silks imported from France. This ensemble is sewn from two fabrics with different patterns, and its elegant combination of three colours is exceptionally effective. It is a truly magnificent suit.

The fabric used for the coat has a green satin ground and features a heavy, symmetrical, stylized pattern, consisting of wide lace garlands and fanciful leaves, flowers and fruit. The colours have faded somewhat over time, but in the pleats at the side the original vivid colour is preserved. The large slit cuffs of the coat and waistcoat are made from a different type of silk, with a pattern consisting of large bouquets with a single large flower resembling a peony in the centre and sharp oval scalloped compartments containing floral compositions in red and green silk and silver thread on a silver background. The main pattern is embellished by garlands composed of small many-petalled rosettes, leaves and bunches of grapes.

Silks that incorporate silver can be very heavy. In this case, the back and the sleeves of the waistcoat are made of plain white silk which would have reduced the overall weight of the garment. The suit is decorated with buttons made of different kinds of silver thread, and the lower part of the waistcoat is trimmed with a complex silver decorative fringe.

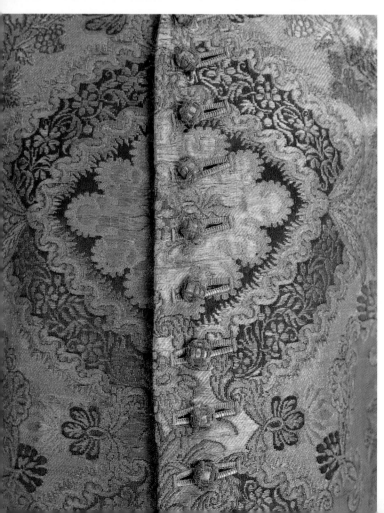

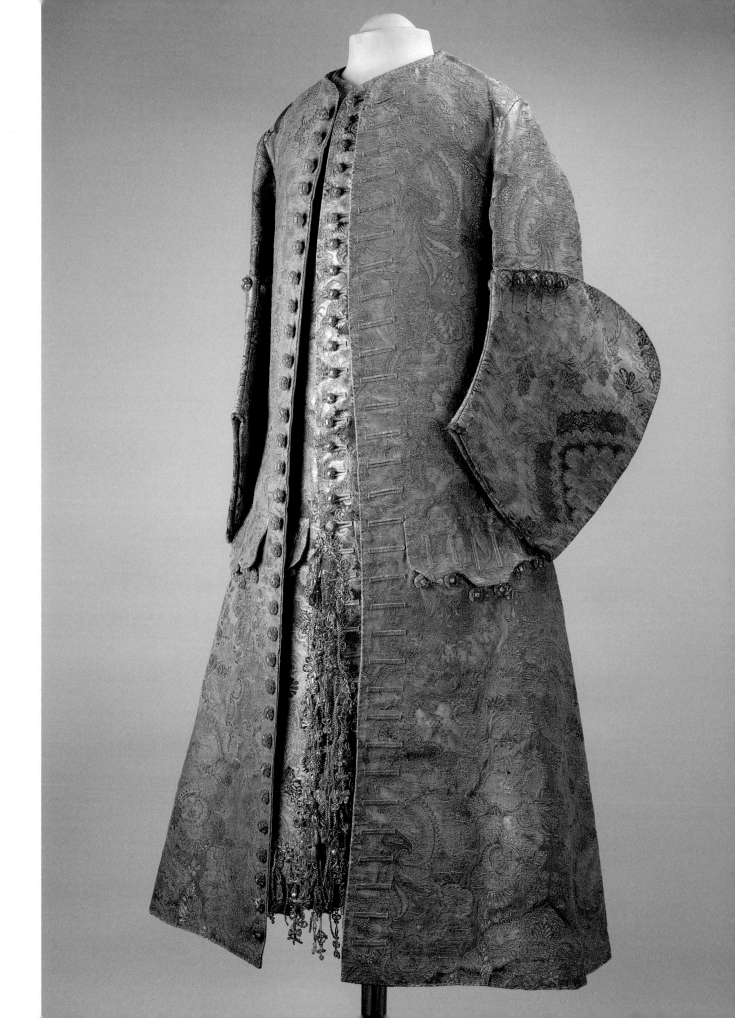

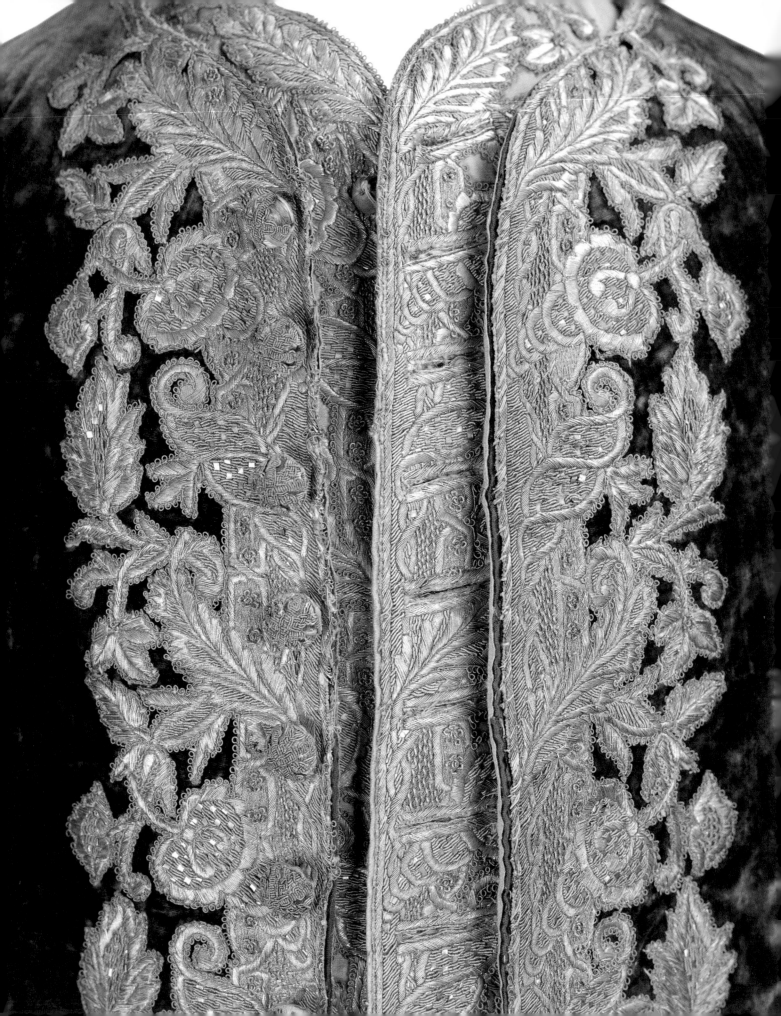

SUIT (*KOSTYUM*), 1727–30

France
TK-1943, TK-2914, TK-1919

THIS is one of five formal suits made from silk velvet in
Peter's wardrobe, and the only one in dark blue. The cuffs,
the lining of the coat and the waistcoat are made from
a silk called *tartsenel* in eighteenth-century Russian
documents. Its delicate pink colour has faded significantly
over time and is preserved in its original form only on the
reverse of the waistcoat cuffs and the pocket flaps.

The main decorative element of this suit is a pattern
embroidered in several types of silver thread, the basis
of which is a stylized floral and foliate ornament. This
embroidery has been worked separately and applied to
the ground, framing the pocket flaps and the coat and
waistcoat cuffs and the openings on the coat and breeches.
The breeches have narrow legs and a full seat, gathered
into the waistband in pleats; they are lined with flannelette.
This volume supported the flared shape of the coat, which
was fashionable at the time. There are four pockets in the
breeches: two in the side seams and two under triangular
flaps on the front. The breeches fasten at the front with
buttons and can be laced tight at the back. The lower edge
of the breeches covers the knee in front, and there is a slit
under the knee at the back.

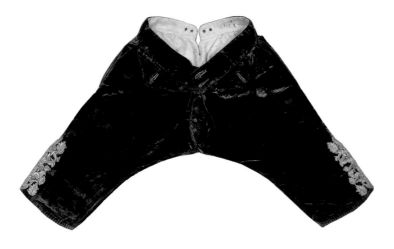

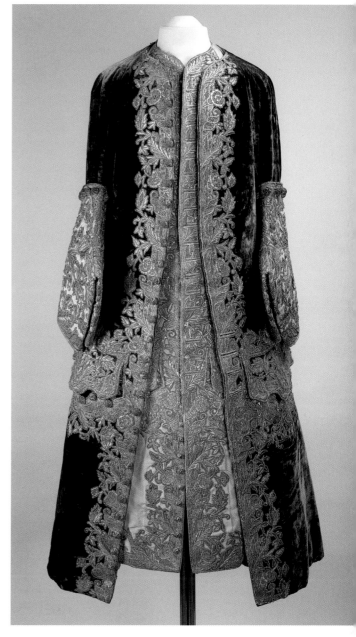

COATS AND WAISTCOATS, 1727–30

France; wool – England
TK-1879, TK-1880, TK-2911, TK-2912

PETER II's wardrobe contains five formal suits for winter, all of which are made of wool with metal embroidery. They are identical in terms of cut but differ in colour and in the pattern of the embroidery, for which silver or gilt thread was used. These kinds of thread were produced for use in different types of embroidery. The technique most commonly used in Russia was couching: silver thread was laid on the surface of the base fabric in the shape of the pattern and then each strand was sewn down with small stitches. The alternative was the technique used for these suits: the silver thread is sewn through the fabric in the shape of the pattern.

The coat and waistcoat of the first ensemble are made in dark-green wool and lined with spotted light-green taffeta. They are decorated with silver embroidery in a pattern made up of undulating lines of ribbon entwined with sprigs of a single large flower and buds. The matching breeches have also been preserved – they are of green wool with matching embroidery and knee bands of silver braid, which fasten with copper buckles.

The second ensemble is made of red wool and is lined with white taffeta. It is decorated with an intricate embroidered pattern in silver thread, in which fanciful motifs, entwined with lace, alternate with floral motifs composed of feathery leaves and small flowers. This is the only formal coat in the wardrobe decorated with the insignia of an Order. The star of the Order of Saint Andrew, which was the highest order of chivalry in the Russian Empire and was headed by the Emperor himself, is sewn onto the front of the coat. This star was probably embroidered in Moscow in the workshop of Baron N.G. Stroganov, where according to the recollections of a well-informed contemporary around 100 girls were engaged in producing embroidery for sale, including 'the finishing of such stars as were worn on the chests of the Knights of Saint Andrew.'[2] The star of the Danish Order of the White Elephant is sewn onto the waistcoat, although there is no documentary evidence that the Emperor was a Knight of this Order. The shoulder of the coat features a loop for the purpose of attaching the sash of the Order. This ensemble may have been worn for ceremonies relating to the feast days of the orders of chivalry, which were held regularly at court during Peter's reign.

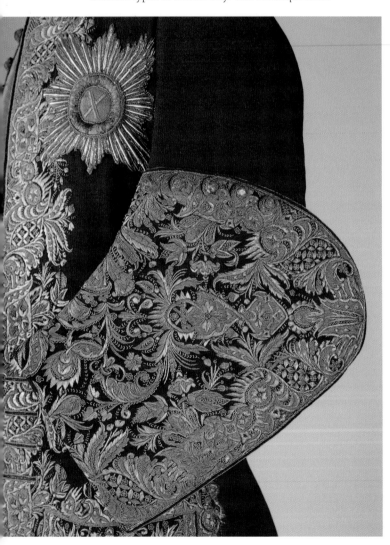

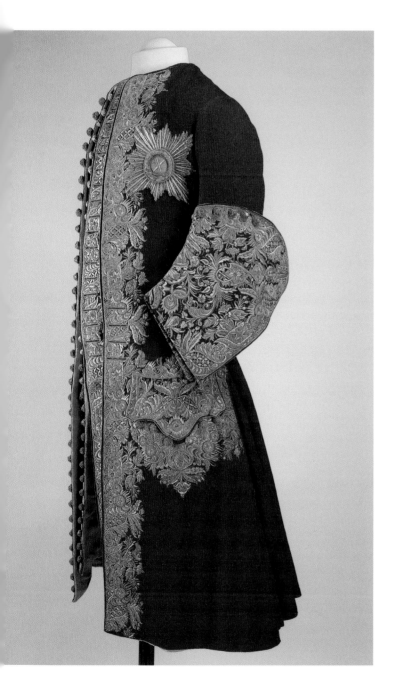

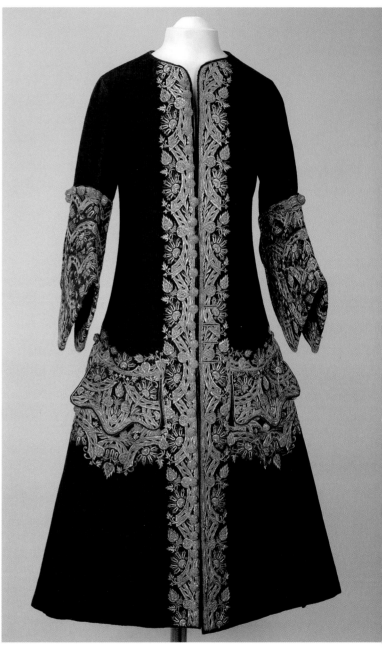

WAISTCOATS, 1727–30

France
TK-1887, TK-1940, TK-1947

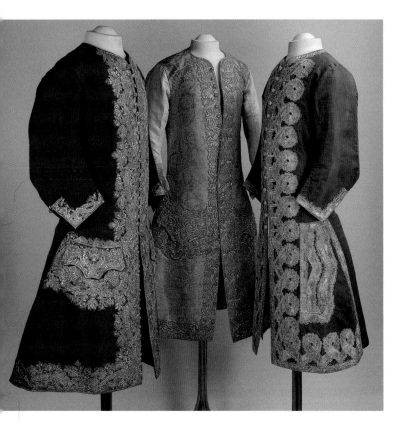

PETER II's wardrobe includes a great variety of elegant waistcoats, which were worn underneath a coat. These waistcoats were cut to fit the upper body snugly, their skirt flared out, the fullness created by three slits from waist to hem. The visible parts – the front of the skirts with their functional pockets and the lower part of the close-fitting sleeves – are decorated to match the coat, and the back and sides are left plain.

The white patterned silk waistcoat, which was worn with a crimson velvet coat lined with silver watered silk, is decorated on the chest and the pocket flaps with silver embroidery. The pattern of this embroidery features shoots with flowers and leaves and decorative ornament. The original trimmings must have been acquired ready-made as they were clearly too large for the garment and in some places are doubled over. The luxurious silk features a foliate pattern made up of small bouquets of flowers with long, thin leaves and large buds and rosettes in fanciful cartouches, and is woven in white silk and silver thread on a silver background. The upper part of the sleeves and the back and lining are made from white silk. The waistcoat is decorated with 41 thread-covered buttons.

The second waistcoat is made entirely from green silk lined with white silk and is decorated with two kinds of silver braid. The waistcoat is part of a set that comprises a camel-coloured cashmere coat with standing collar and vertical flaps on the pockets and sleeves and matching breeches. This suit is unique in Peter's wardrobe in that the decorative effect is provided not by the outer garment, which is modestly decorated with silver buttons and buttonholes, but by the waistcoat – even the side slits are trimmed with braid.

The red silk waistcoat was designed to be worn with a coat and breeches made of light-blue wool. All three pieces are decorated with embroidery worked in two kinds of silver thread and consisting of a heavy foliate ornament with fanciful flowers and leaves, and ornamental compositions. The pattern of this embroidery is identical to that on the waistcoat from the Emperor's coronation ensemble (see p.25), which indicates that both outfits were probably made at the same time and that the embroidery may have come from the same workshop. However, unlike the coronation ensemble, this waistcoat was worn more than once and even underwent adjustments (it has been let out at the side seams). As it was originally made for the 12-year-old Emperor, he probably soon grew out of it.

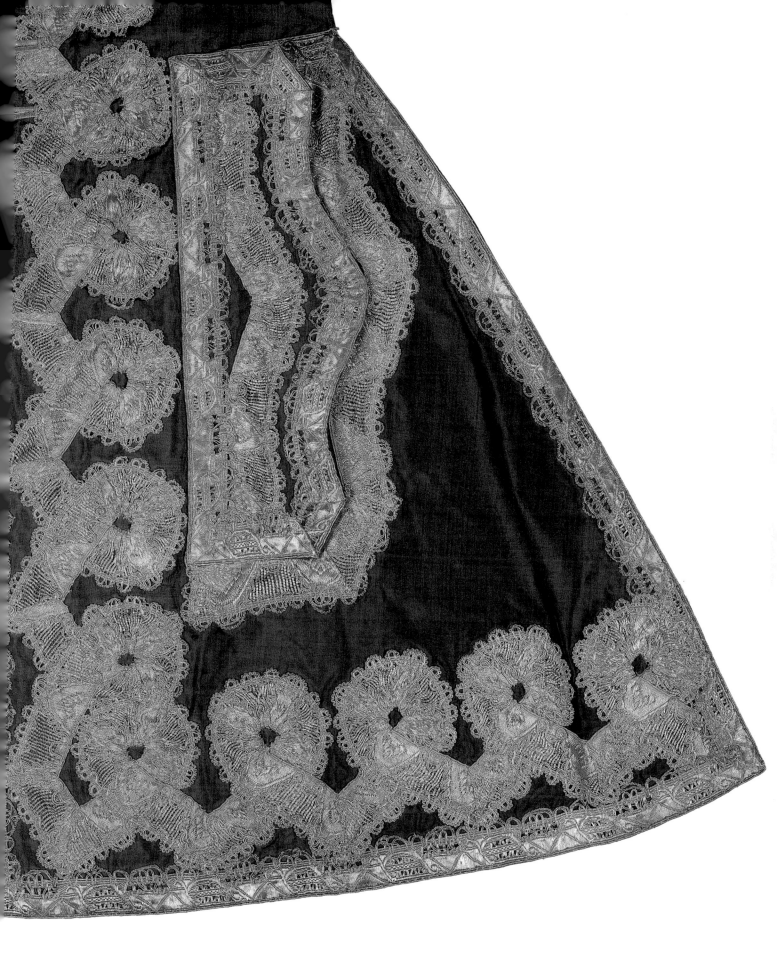

MOURNING COAT, 1727
Russia
TK-2607

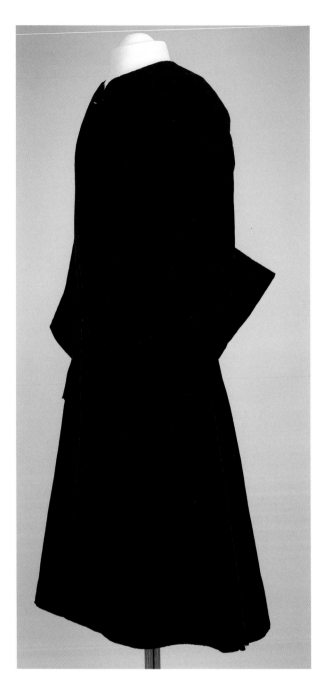

THIS black coat was worn for mourning, black attire having
been prescribed by an old Russian tradition long before
the reforms of Peter the Great. From the beginning of the
eighteenth century, imitation of Western European styles
began taking place not only for daily but also for ritual events.
Mourning required a specific form of dress with minimal
decoration and was subject to strict regulations in terms of
the choice of fabric. Black wool or silk velvet was to be worn
for the period of full mourning. After some time it was also
possible to wear other more lustrous types of black silk,
and during the period of half mourning grey, white and silver
were permitted.

Peter's wardrobe contains eight black suits whose fabric
and decoration indicate that they were made for different
periods of mourning. Three are made from wool and have
a warm lining so were probably for the winter months. Two
lighter suits are made from a textured plain silk and lined
with taffeta, and are fastened with silk buttons in the form
of thorns. Two velvet suits offer the most striking indication
of the decorations and colour combinations permitted in
dress according to the period of mourning. One is made
entirely from black velvet and lined with black taffeta; even
the knee bands with steel buckles on the breeches are black.
The second probably belongs to the category of half
mourning: the velvet coat is lined with silver watered silk
and decorated with cuffs of silver brocade, silver buttons
and buttonholes; the waistcoat is made entirely from silver
brocade and trimmed with a silver fringe along the hem.

This coat of black wool with a ribbed wool lining is
the most severe of all being completely devoid of decoration.
Its five buttons, which are covered with black wool, are
exclusively functional. This coat is part of a set that also
comprises wool waistcoat and breeches.

Unlike most of the Emperor's full dress ensembles, his
mourning attire shows evidence of heavy wear. During Peter's
short reign, there were two periods of mourning at court:
the first for Catherine I and the second for his elder and only
sister Grand Duchess Natalya Alexeevna. One of the Spanish

envoy's reports noted that on 31 December 1728 a period
of 'the strictest mourning [was announced] for the late Grand
Duchess, whose body was displayed to the public with great
splendour. Mourning lasted for eight months and applied not
only to staff but also to carriages and dwellings.'³ Seven of
Peter's mourning suits were made for this period, while this
coat was made when he was younger and smaller.

OFFICER'S COAT AND HAT OF THE SEMENOVSKY LIFE GUARDS REGIMENT, 1727–30

Russia
TK-1979, TK-2755

UNIFORMS make up a significant part of Peter's wardrobe. A number of these uniforms were intended for hunting and riding, while the remainder are examples of the military uniform of the Russian Guards.

The first uniform regulations, which were introduced in 1720, dictated the colours of the uniforms to be worn by different troops according to their regiment and rank. Officers of two regiments of the Russian Imperial Guard – the Preobrazhensky and Semenovsky Regiments – were accorded identical dark-green uniforms, which differed only in the positioning of their gold braid.

On this Semenovsky Life Guards uniform coat, the braid edges the skirts, cuffs, collar and pocket flaps. The coat is lined with green velvet. The waistcoat, made from identical wool that goes with this coat, is decorated with braid and gilded bronze buttons and lined with white taffeta. Judging by the pattern and positioning of its braid, a black hat – one of nine in Peter's wardrobe – also goes with this ensemble.

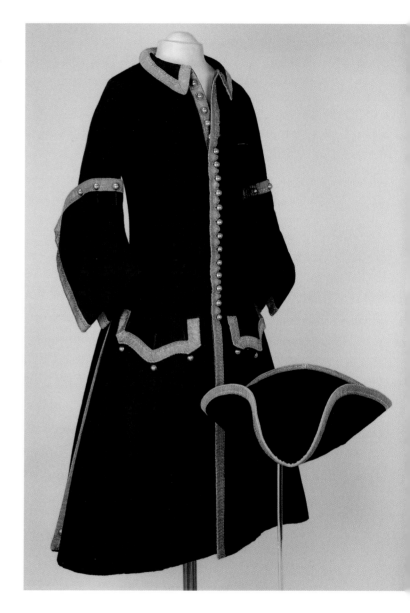

NIGHTGOWNS (*SHLAFROKI*), 1727–30

Silk – France
TK-2379, TK-2380

INFORMAL robes, similar in style to the long-skirted coats dating to before Peter the Great's reforms, became popular amongst the Russian élite at the beginning of the eighteenth century and were known as *shlafroki* or *shlafory*, from the German *Schlafrock* (dressing gown – or in the eighteenth century, nightgown). They were made from expensive plain or patterned fabric – satin, taffeta, damask or brocade. The nightgowns varied according to season: warm ones were lined with ermine, sable, squirrel or lynx fur or quilted with wadding, and lighter ones were lined with silk. They were worn at home, being loose-fitting and comfortable but at the same time smart and impressive enough for receiving distinguished guests. Some witnesses noted that in some cases these nightgowns even bore stars of the orders. Documentary sources indicate that two different kinds of nightgowns were popular in the first third of the eighteenth century. Both are included within Peter's wardrobe.

The more traditional variant is represented by the Eastern-style T-shaped nightgown with wide sleeves, made from whole loom widths of white brocaded damask imported from France: linear undulating garlands made up of little vases of flowers and leafy tendrils are woven in gilt thread and coloured silk on the white damask ground, which features a curvaceous pattern of leaves and fruits, flanked by wide stripes with indentations. The considerable width of the hem of the nightgown is achieved though the V-shaped inserts at the sides. The yellow taffeta lining is quilted in parallel lines.

The second nightgown, made in Prussian style, would have been something of a fashion novelty in Russia during Peter's reign. It is full-length, drawn in at the waist and flares sharply at the side and behind; it fastens on both sides (is double-breasted). The narrow sleeves are decorated with buttoned flaps. This is obviously one of the warm nightgowns, as beneath the yellow taffeta lining there is a heavy wool interlining. The gown itself is made of a distinctive sky blue patterned silk with a white design.

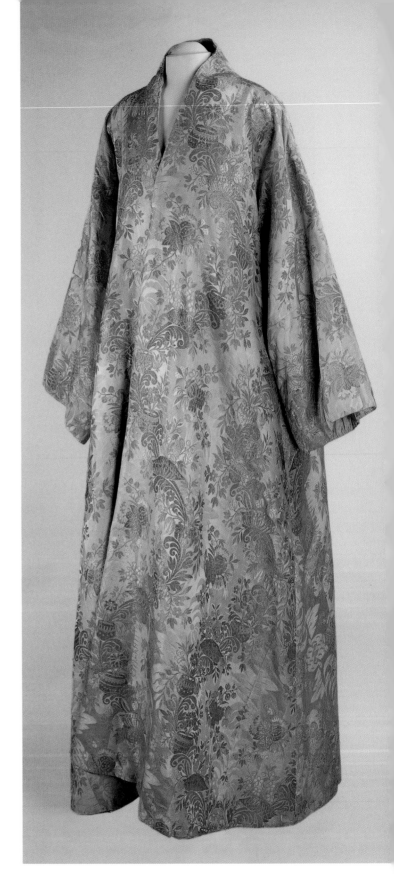

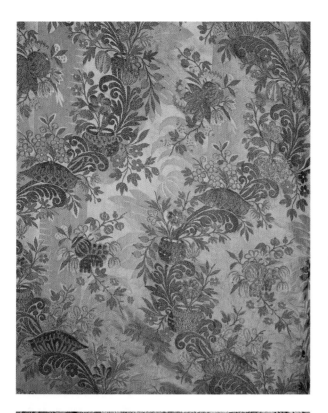

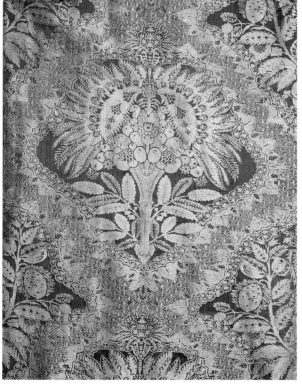

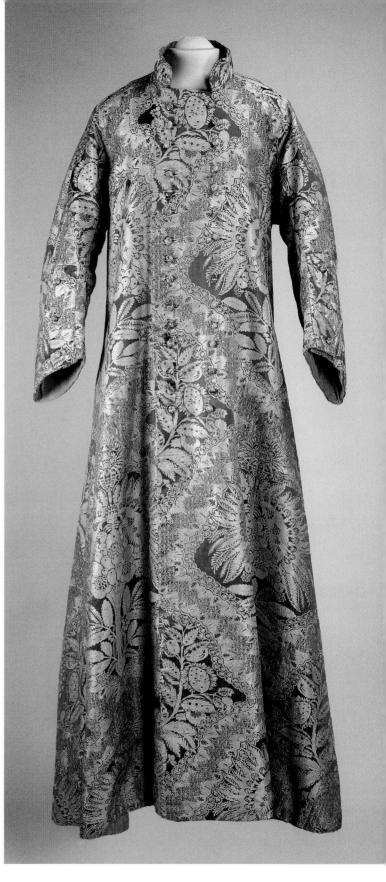

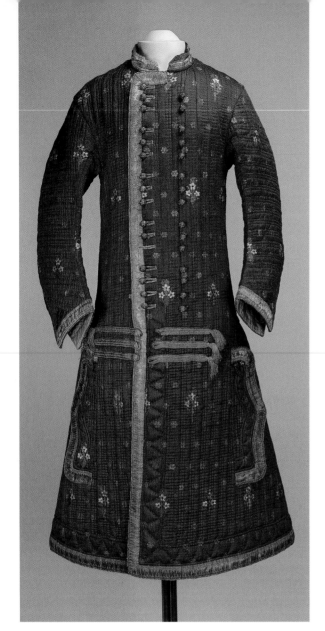

BANYAN (*BESHMET*), 1727–30
Fabric – Iran
TK-2590

A SPECIAL group in Peter's wardrobe consists of three Eastern-style banyans. These robes are identical in cut and are made of silk fabric in varying shades of red. One is made from plain satin, and the other two are made of patterned fabric with small floral motifs. The banyans may have been brought from the East as ambassadorial gifts for the Emperor, either as made-up garments or as lengths of silk. The silk lining and silver braid are, however, of Western European manufacture, so the garments combine luxury fashion textiles from different parts of the world. They represent the Western European taste for Eastern exotica.

The name given to these robes in Russian – *beshmet* – is of Turkish origin. These double-breasted, quilted banyans are drawn in at the waist, sharply flared and lined with coloured linen. They have narrow sleeves and a standing collar and fasten by means of small buttons arranged in groups of three or four. A distinctive feature of this type of robe was the fastening on both sides, which meant that it was possible to increase the size as necessary. This was possible because although one of the skirts is straight, the other features a 4cm (1¹⁄₂ in) wide vertical rectangular slit beginning under the fifth group of buttons and running right down to the hem. The buttons above the slit fasten with cut buttonholes, whereas the group of three buttons below, which are sewn right to the very edge of both skirts at the same level, fasten with loops formed of horizontal strips of silver braid with tassels at the ends. When the straight skirt is fastened, the buttonhole-strips on this skirt play a purely decorative role; when the skirt with the slit is fastened (thereby decreasing the size of the garment), the buttonhole strips on this side come into play. The fact that it was possible to increase the size of the *beshmet* indicates that this garment was multi-functional.

In the inventory of Peter's wardrobe, banyans were listed in the category of domestic attire. However, there is reason to believe that *beshmety* were worn in the East, where they originated, as an outdoor garment worn underneath a heavy coat. Only their front is decorated, ornamental flaps covering vertical pocket slits. In contrast, the slits in the side seams are purely functional and devoid of any decoration, giving access to the pockets in the breeches. They were not visible when a coat was worn on top of the banyan. For the same reason, the front hem was trimmed only as far as the side seams.

This *beshmet*, lined with yellow taffeta, is considerably better preserved than the other two in Peter's wardrobe, and is also decorated more richly: the buttons are covered with silver rather than silk braid, and the collar, the edge of the skirt, the front hem and the pocket flaps are trimmed with patterned braid instead of plain silver cord. The beshmet is made from red satin, and its pattern is woven in fine gilt thread and dark-blue and white silk.

WAISTCOAT (*DUSHEGREYA*), 1727–30

Silk – France (?)
TK-2586

ONE of the most popular items of men's indoor dress for the Russian aristocracy in the first third of the eighteenth century was the *dushegreya*, or 'soul-warmer'. The name *dushegreya* was borrowed from the lexicon of traditional national costume and applied to jackets or waistcoats of varying length. The wardrobe of His Highness Prince A.D. Menshikov, the most influential grandee of the State and to all intents and purposes regent for the young Emperor at the beginning of his reign, contained 37 examples, approximately half of which had trimmings. *Dushegrei* were made from a great variety of fabrics, including wool, linen, flannelette and silk (taffeta, satin, damask, velvet, brocade), although preference was shown for taffeta and satin. Judging by their name, *dushegrei* were intended for warmth, though they were further subdivided into seasonal variants, the warm ones being quilted or lined with fur. Most of them were sleeveless and fastened with hooks or buttons.

There are five *dushegrei* in Peter's wardrobe, three of which are tailored in a similar way to waistcoats. One of these is made of scarlet satin and is lined with fine linen and fastens with ribbons; the second, made from camel-coloured wool, is double-breasted and fastens with buttons on both sides; and the third, with similar fastening, is made of high-quality imported yellow silk shot with white and lined with linen. The remaining two *dushegrei* are in the style of shortened jackets drawn in at the waist and have detachable sleeves, which attach to the armholes with silk ribbons.

This little *dushegreya* is made of silk, which was originally crimson but has faded considerably. It is lined with white taffeta and interlined for warmth with white wool. There are small slits at the bottom of the side seams and four overstitched eyelets on the armholes and sleeves where they lace together. The double-breasted fastening features 18 buttons, which are covered with the main fabric. The sleeves have slits at the wrist with button fastenings. Another *dushegreya* in the collection has lost its sleeves but is in the same style and is lined with squirrel fur. It was probably made to be worn during winter.

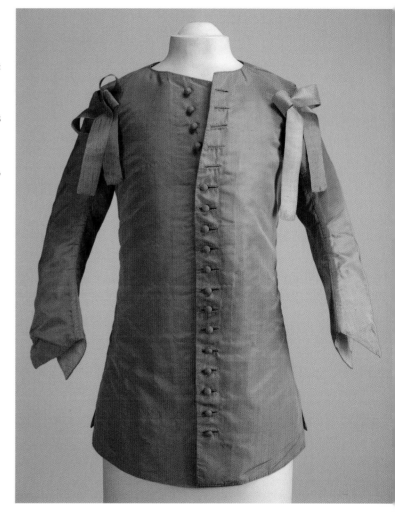

SHIRT (*SOROCHKA*), 1727–30
Linen – Holland (?)
TK-1930

PETER'S wardrobe contains several very rare examples of men's undergarments, which are all made of fine linen. As well as the shirt and drawers given to the Armoury as part of the young Emperor's coronation ensemble, the collection includes two further shirts, which differ in length and in the style of the collar, cuffs and side slits. One is quite short and features a narrow standing collar and wide cuffs; this shirt was obviously for everyday wear as it is very heavily worn, with numerous repairs and patches. The second is knee-length.

This shirt is basically T-shaped, the body made from a single length of fabric and the sleeves from a single length of fabric sewn on to the body. Each sleeve is gathered at the cuff in tiny pleats, demonstrating the exceptional skill of the seamstress. The narrow cuffs are finished with long buttonholes through which ribbons or some kind of button fastening were probably inserted.

The collar of the shirt is typical of eighteenth-century construction: a horizontal slit has been made in the centre of the shoulder fold, and almost the entire width of the panel is closely gathered around it. The base of the vertical front neck opening is strengthened by an ornamented inset in the form of a heart. The high standing collar, which was worn folded down, has two buttonholes cut in front near the seam.

Due to the archaic cut of undergarments of this period, which differed fundamentally from the cut of the outer garments, special techniques were adopted to reinforce the linen. Triangular underarm gussets were sewn into all shirts, the shoulder panel was strengthened either with additional strips of fabric or by means of triangular inserts, and the lower side slits were strengthened by square strips sewn crosswise.

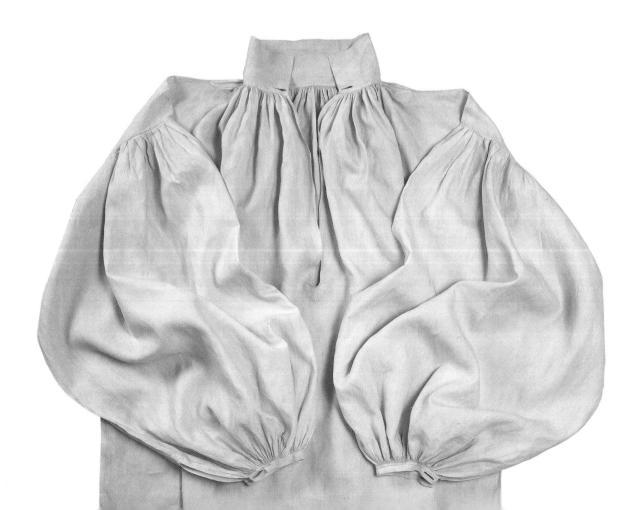

GAITERS (*SHTIBLETY*), 1727–30

Russia (?)
TK-1903/1-2

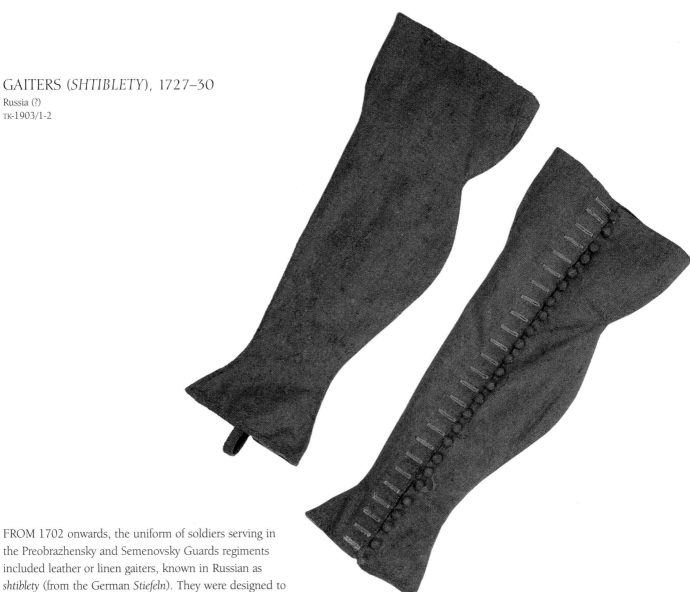

FROM 1702 onwards, the uniform of soldiers serving in the Preobrazhensky and Semenovsky Guards regiments included leather or linen gaiters, known in Russian as *shtiblety* (from the German *Stiefeln*). They were designed to be worn over stockings in campaign conditions. During the first quarter of the eighteenth century, woollen gaiters were often also worn over shoes in bad weather. In 1729, a particularly cold winter led to a fashion in France for high buttoned woollen gaiters, which were subsequently adopted in hunting attire.[4] Peter's wardrobe contains a pair of grey wool gaiters of this type, which are lined with white linen and feature fastening strips and 25 wool-covered wooden buttons on the outside of the leg. Despite his youth the Emperor thoroughly enjoyed hunting, and the signs of heavy wear – the broken fastening strips and traces of blacking on the lower part of the lining – indicate that these gaiters were probably part of his hunting attire.

Peter started going hunting in the area surrounding Moscow immediately after his coronation, having developed a passion for this pursuit under the influence of his 19-year-old chamberlain and favourite Prince I.A. Dolgoruky. He spent much of his short reign in the forest, on the field and at hunting camps. 'Hunting', wrote the English diplomat Claude Rondeau in August 1728, 'is the predominant passion of the Tsar.' His hunting expeditions usually lasted from 10 to 26 days, but in July and August 1729 he set an unusual record when he was away hunting for 55 days continuously. Only heavy snowfalls or freezing conditions could force him to return to Moscow, and even then not for long. However, in Autumn 1729 Peter and his retinue with a pack of 600 hounds caught 4,000 hares, 50 foxes, five lynx and three bears,[5] after which the Emperor appears to have tired of hunting and given away many of his dogs.

STOCKINGS (*CHULKI*), 1727–30
Western Europe
ТК-209/1-2, ТК-210/1-2

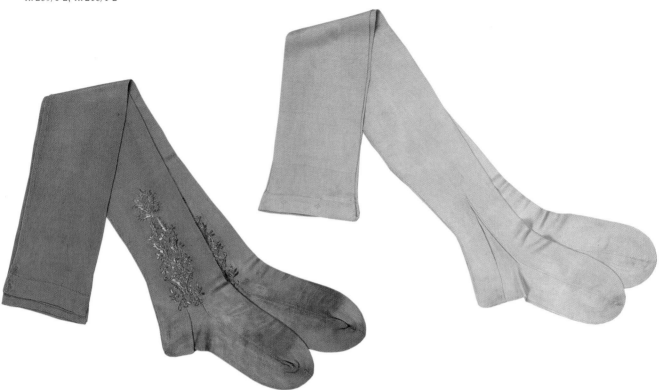

AS early as the second half of the seventeenth century, silk and wool knitted stockings were being imported into Russia from Europe in such quantity that they were evidently being worn not only by foreigners but also by local residents.[6] The traditional variety were hand-made stockings, which had been worn by the most privileged members of society for centuries and managed to survive the dress reforms. These were most often made from red silk, and winter stockings were additionally lined with fox, deer or wolf fur.[7]

Knitted stockings were first manufactured in Russia during the reign of Peter the Great, at a silk textile workshop founded in Moscow in 1717. The owners of the workshop – F.A. Apraksin, P.A. Tolstoy and P.P. Shafirov – were important statesmen and were granted a government subsidy to purchase equipment and the right to duty-free trade for 50 years.[8] Unfortunately, no detailed information has yet been found concerning either the quality or the range of production at this workshop. For the coronation of Empress Catherine I in 1724, stockings for the full dress ensembles of courtiers taking part in the ceremony were ordered abroad: the 24 footmen wore red worsted stockings from

England, and the coachmen and postilions wore red stockings with gold embroidery from Venice.[9]

The 25 pairs of knitted stockings in Peter's wardrobe are rare examples of men's dress accessories manufactured in the first third of the eighteenth century. Four pairs are of white and grey silk, embroidered in silver or gilt thread; three pairs are of white silk with ornament on the sides (clocks); two pairs are of black worsted without decoration; and 16 pairs are of thick white loosely twisted thread.

The long knitted grey silk stockings have a tailored sole and a vertical seam at the back, and the tops are turned over and stitched down to form a hem with an opening on the inside. Every single one of the Emperor's silk stockings features a similar hem and opening: a ribbon was probably threaded through the latter to act as a kind of internal garter. The pattern on the clocks embroidered in gilt thread consists of coiled leafy shoots. The second pair of stockings is knitted from white silk, their decoration on the sides featuring two wavy lines topped by an ornamental figure. The quality of both pairs of stockings clearly indicates that they were intended to be worn with full dress attire.

GLOVES (*PERCHATKI*), 1727–30

Western Europe
TK-217/1-2

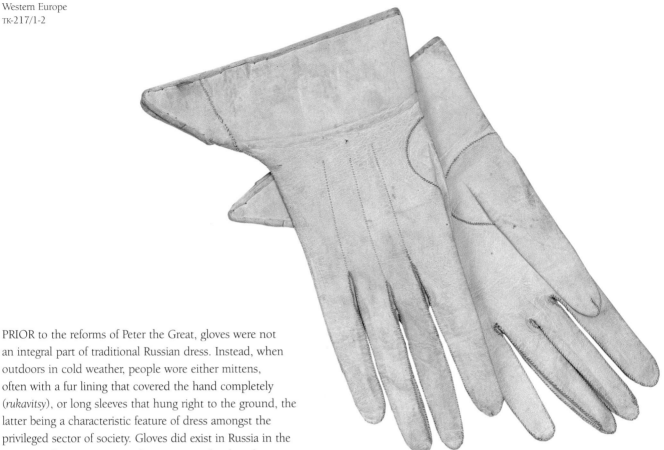

PRIOR to the reforms of Peter the Great, gloves were not an integral part of traditional Russian dress. Instead, when outdoors in cold weather, people wore either mittens, often with a fur lining that covered the hand completely (*rukavitsy*), or long sleeves that hung right to the ground, the latter being a characteristic feature of dress amongst the privileged sector of society. Gloves did exist in Russia in the seventeenth century, primarily in court circles, but they were a rare imported luxury and were given to the Russian Tsars as ambassadorial gifts from the countries of Western Europe, including England. The Armoury collection includes several pairs of gloves, including those of knitted silk and chamois leather, and embroidered in silver and coloured silk.

The official introduction of Western European style dress into Russia at the beginning of the eighteenth century made the use of gloves essential, even though for a long time fine, high-quality leather gloves could only be obtained abroad. For the coronation of Catherine I in 1724, white gloves for her 12 pages were ordered in Berlin, and every year 360 pairs of 'the best plain and kidskin gloves, renowned throughout Europe' were bought for Empress Elizabeth Petrovna in Sweden from a factory 'where only they were made.' In 1751, this factory closed and reopened in the city of Malmö; however, by this point the Empress was no longer satisfied with the quality of its work and decided to stop buying finished gloves and instead to buy the leather and hire a master craftsman to make them to order. This responsibility was assigned to leather

manufacturer Sigismund Dunckel, who had been operating a leatherworks at the Kipensky farmstead near the village of Kipen and Gorky in the Konorsky *uyezd*. In 1752, he 'managed to process glove leather of such quality as had never before been made in Russia, and which was as good as any foreign sample', and thereafter he successfully supplied gloves to the court for a number of years.[10]

Peter's wardrobe contains 20 pairs of identical fine white leather gloves and two pairs of chamois leather gloves. Each pair features slit gauntlets, interlined with parchment and covered with leather binding. Customs stamps in sealing-wax inside these gauntlets indicate that they were all imported. The gloves are sewn with the seam on the outside, with three points stitched in silk and triangular inserts between the fingers. Most of the gloves appear to have never been worn, since they are not at all stretched or creased. The fine silk thread has gradually weakened over the course of the last 300 years and many of the gloves have come partially unstitched at the seams.

Weapons and Jewellery

Of the various items of luxury distinguishing the Russian nobility, nothing astonishes the foreign visitor quite so much as the abundance of precious stones that shine on different parts of their dress. In most European countries, these expensive decorations are almost exclusively worn by women (with the exception of a few of the most distinguished or richest individuals), but in Russia men compete in this regard with their female counterparts. Many of the noblemen are covered in diamonds from head to toe – their buttons, buckles and epaulettes are all set with diamonds, as are the hilts of their swords, and their hats are frequently studded with several rows of them. Even stars made of diamonds are commonplace here.[1]

THESE comments from the famous English traveller and historian William Coxe, who visited Russia twice in the last quarter of the eighteenth century, convey a sense of the extravagance and incomparable luxury that prevailed in the Russian court and which had begun to consume a significant and increasing part of the State budget. Living in grand style was fashionable at the time and corresponded to the aesthetic taste of the era, when the wealth and splendour of the court was considered a measure of the wealth and might of the Empire. In order to gain favour with the monarch, it was necessary to spend vast sums on one's wardrobe. Finding the means to stand out from the gilded crowd filling the palace apartments often meant selling hundreds of serfs every year.

Men's full court dress of the eighteenth century required numerous accessories, each serving a different purpose. Elegant jewelled pins could be fastened on a lace cravat or the brim of a hat, and buckles encrusted with precious stones were used to fasten shoes and breeches. Gold, silver or jewelled buttons often adorned coats and waistcoats, which were woven with silver and covered with intricate patterns, and gold chatelaines bearing watches and trinkets hung at the waist.

Some fashionable men even had a specific sword, buckles, signet ring and snuffbox to match each of their many outfits. Snuffboxes in particular were considered an indispensable accessory and were carried everywhere. They were by far the most popular gift and the most prestigious Imperial award for much of the eighteenth century in Russia. Owning a snuffbox given by the Emperor came to be recognized as an unmistakable sign of Imperial favour. Notes were sent inside snuffboxes, which consequently became known as 'love letter boxes'. Some artful card-sharps even used their snuffboxes to make their fortune: they would carefully polish the gold or enamel surface of their snuffbox before standing it in front of them on the card table and contriving to catch the reflection of the cards as they were dealt out over it.

Viewing other people's snuffbox collections was a popular pastime, almost a social obligation. Snuffboxes were displayed for guests on shelves and special tables. In the study of the fashionable society gentleman they lay on the desk amongst papers and fripperies. The finest artists and jewellers of the day specialized in the creation of snuffboxes, and these lavish knick-knacks, made of gold and silver, inlaid with mother of pearl and covered with precious stones were frequently worth a small fortune. The inside or outside of the lid often featured a portrait of the owner's family, close friend or his beloved monarch,

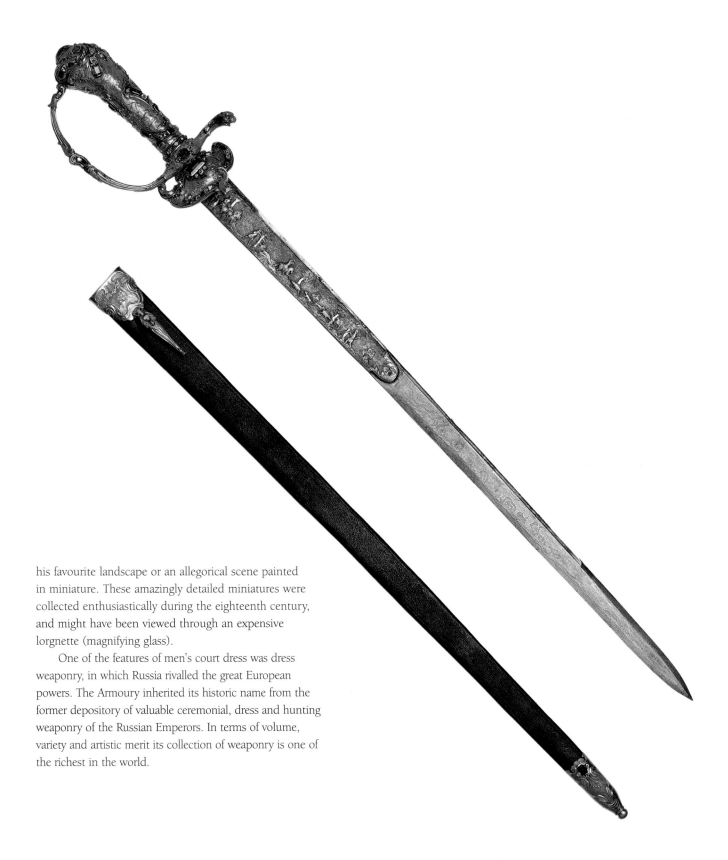

his favourite landscape or an allegorical scene painted in miniature. These amazingly detailed miniatures were collected enthusiastically during the eighteenth century, and might have been viewed through an expensive lorgnette (magnifying glass).

One of the features of men's court dress was dress weaponry, in which Russia rivalled the great European powers. The Armoury inherited its historic name from the former depository of valuable ceremonial, dress and hunting weaponry of the Russian Emperors. In terms of volume, variety and artistic merit its collection of weaponry is one of the richest in the world.

HUNTING SWORD IN SHEATH, MID-18TH CENTURY

Russia (?)
OR-2243/1-2

RICHLY decorated swords and daggers were used in Russia not only for hunting but also as accessories for full formal dress. The lavish ornamentation of this sword (see also p.73), which is encrusted with 143 diamonds and 58 large emeralds of the highest quality, indicates that it belonged to a particularly high-ranking individual. The steel blade is decorated with scenes of wild-boar hunting, and the gold hilt and guard are decorated with scenes of falconry and course hunting. It is thought that this sword was sent on 16 April 1747 to the palace at Oranienbaum – the summer residence of the heir to the Russian throne, the future Emperor Peter III, and his spouse Catherine Alexeevna – by Empress Elizabeth Petrovna. Until the end of the reign of Catherine the Great, the sword was kept in a diamond workshop attached to the court before being transferred in 1798 to the Rustkammer in Saint Petersburg and then in 1810 to the Moscow Armoury.

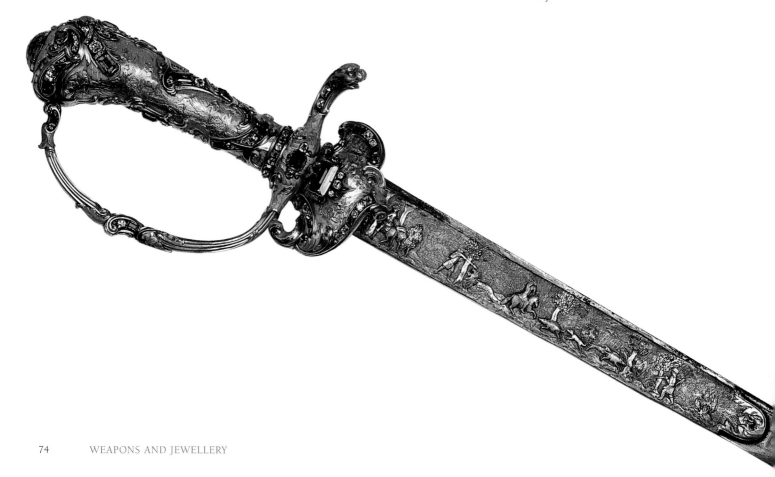

GUNPOWDER FLASK (*NATRUSKA*), MID-18TH CENTURY

Russia
OR-2244

THIS gold flask, set with 294 diamonds, was designed to store gunpowder. Such flasks were part of hunting attire and were worn on a shoulder strap on the right-hand side of the body. One side is decorated with the State Emblem of the Russian Empire, and the other features the monogram of Empress Elizabeth Petrovna. This unique piece comes from the weaponry collection of Emperor Peter III and was probably given to him by Empress Elizabeth Petrovna in April 1747. It was kept initially at his residence in Oranienbaum (in the Oranienbaum Rustkammer) and later in the Saint Petersburg Rustkammer.

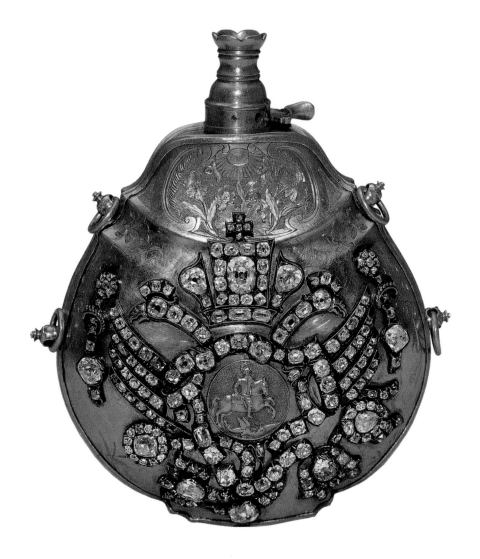

POCKET TELESCOPE, MID-18TH CENTURY

Western Europe
DK-1429

THIS cylindrical optical instrument is a telescope consisting of two parts that screw together, with sliding lens covers. The telescope case is made of heliotrope or red jasper, mounted in gold and overlaid with pierced bands of flowers, leaves, tendrils and the graceful figures of dolphins. The case also features the Latin letters 'GAGR', which are in silver relief and set with diamonds and rubies. Judging by its small size and luxurious setting, this telescope was meant for use at the theatre. When it was given to the Armoury in 1926, the director of the museum at the time, D.D. Ivanov, suggested that the initials stood for Graf (Count) Alexey Grigor'evich Razumovsky (1709–71), who began using this title in 1744 after being awarded the title of *Reichsgraf* by the German Emperor Karl VI.

A.G. Razumovsky, the son of a peasant from Little Russia (Malorossiya), was blessed with outstanding vocal gifts and came to the Imperial Court in 1731 as a member of the court choir. Empress Elizabeth Petrovna was so charmed by the young man's talent and good looks that she made him her favourite and, according to legend, secretly married him after her accession. A.G. Razumovsky enjoyed an unrivalled position at court, where he inspired and nurtured a passion for music and singing. Singers and musicians from Little Russia began flocking to Saint Petersburg, and troupes from Germany and France visited the city on tour, performing theatre, opera, ballet and Commedia dell'arte. A permanent Italian opera was established, and it was during this period that the foundations were laid for a national professional theatre. In 1756, Russia's first permanent public theatre opened in the Imperial capital under the direction of the eminent representative of Russian literature A.P. Sumarokov, whose patron was A.G. Razumovsky.

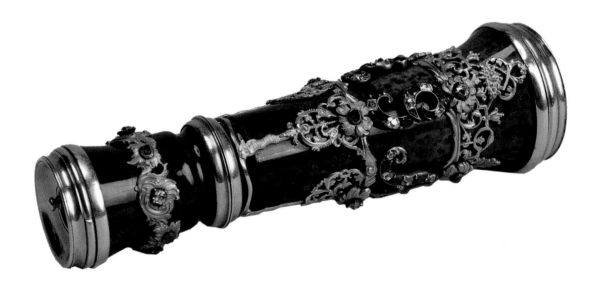

SNUFFBOX, MID-18TH CENTURY

Saint Petersburg
IMPERIAL PORCELAIN FACTORY
F-1928

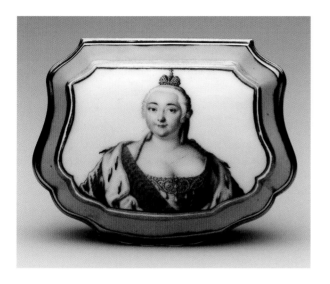

THIS porcelain snuffbox is set in silver and decorated with glazed multi-coloured painting. Its shape was characteristic of the mid-eighteenth century, and the celadon colour of the lid was also highly fashionable at the time. The top of the hinged lid depicts Empress Elizabeth Petrovna wearing a small crown and mantle. To be awarded a snuffbox with a portrait of the crown-wearer in eighteenth-century Russia was an exceptional honour, in some instances even more so than being awarded an Order, and this snuffbox would have been highly valued by its recipient.

The miniature formal portrait is full of expression and shows the Empress, who was famed for her beauty, looking particularly regal. The images of naval battles inside the lid, on the sides and base of the snuffbox indicate that it was made to commemorate a Russian naval victory, as the Russian ships are portrayed sinking the enemy vessels. The insignia of the Order of Saint Andrew on the base of the snuffbox is equally significant: during the reign of Elizabeth Petrovna, this order – the highest order of chivalry of the Russian Empire – was only awarded for particularly eminent services to the Fatherland and the Empress. As head of the order, the Empress is represented

on the snuffbox wearing its light-blue sash.

This snuffbox was one of the personal belongings of Emperor Nicholas II and Empress Alexandra Feodorovna and was kept in their private apartments in the Winter Palace in Saint Petersburg 'in a corner display unit in the Office of Empress Alexandra Feodorovna, between the window and the door leading to the bedroom.'[2] In September 1917, it was sent to the Armoury together with other valuable items that had been rescued from the Imperial palaces. In 1922, during the selection of items from the palace for the Russian State Repository for precious metals and gems, this snuffbox was recognized as having exceptional historical significance and was thus allowed to remain in the museum and was later included in the Armoury collection.[3]

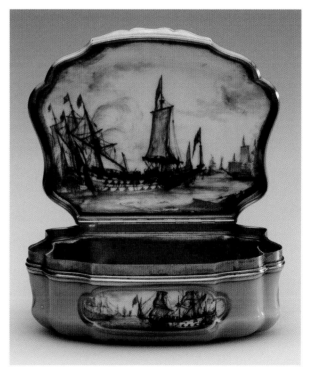

SNUFFBOX, 1754–61

Western Europe
MINIATURE — RUSSIA
MZ-4129

THIS gold snuffbox, inlaid with mother of pearl beneath pierced work, is decorated with relief images of twisting branches, flowers, fruits and insects worked in enamel on gold. On the inside of the lid, there is a miniature portrait under glass of Grand Duke Peter Feodorovich (the future Peter III) in full dress general's uniform of the Holstein regiment. Having inherited the title Duke Holstein-Gottorp from his father, Peter Feodorovich kept it even when he became heir to the throne and later Emperor, and part of the Holstein troops were billeted at his residence in Oranienbaum. According to the memoirs of his wife, the future Catherine the Great, he wore the Holstein uniform at first 'only in his private rooms, and secretly,' but from 1754 he was already wearing 'no other, except to balls, although he was a

lieutenant-colonel of the Preobrazhensky Regiment and, furthermore, was head of the Kirasirsky Regiment in Russia.'[4] In the portrait, the marshal's baton and knight's helmet with feathers portray the Grand Duke as a military leader, while the crimson (as opposed to Imperial gold) mantle lying nearby with the helmet indicates that the portrait was painted before he acceded to the Russian throne.

The miniature bears a close resemblance to the formal portrait of the Grand Duke painted in 1758 by the artist F.S. Rokotov. The favourite of Empress Elizabeth Petrovna, founder of Moscow's university and founder and first president of the Academy of Artists, art collector I.I. Shuvalov was Rokotov's main patron and taught him in his own home under the direction of Pietro Rotari.

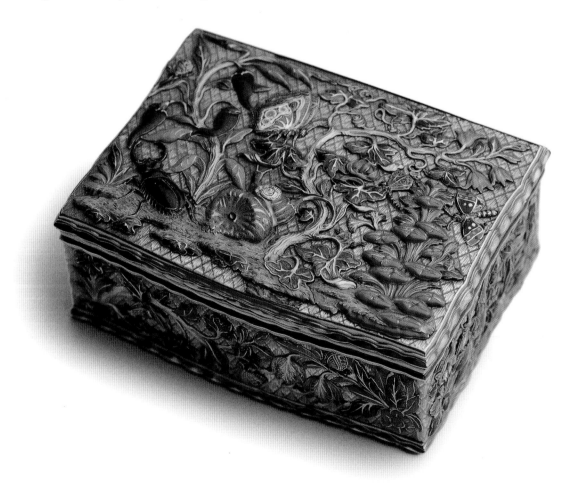

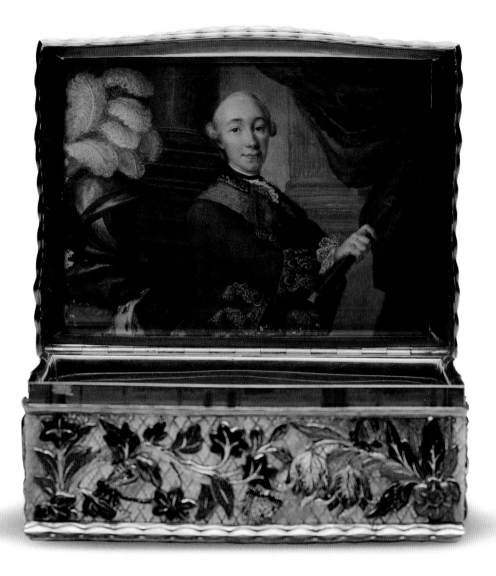

This snuffbox comes from the collection of the famous Shuvalov family, who were loyal supporters of Empress Elizabeth Petrovna and Peter Feodorovich. At the beginning of the twentieth century, it formed part of the collection of Countess E.V. Shuvalova[5] at her palace in Saint Petersburg,[6] where she had a picture gallery and museum. In 1917, the Countess gave two display cases' worth of jewellery, fans and snuffboxes to the Moscow Pawnshop[7] in the hope that they would be safe there; however, after the October Revolution, the deposit was used as the basis for the Russian State Repository for precious metals and gems and all deposits were confiscated from their former owners. When the

snuffbox was given to the Armoury in 1926, a printed ticket was found inside it bearing the coat of arms of the Shuvalov family and the inscription: 'Ticket for masked ball on the 26th day of October 1754. To Katerina Alexandrovna Golovkina.'[8]

Princess K.A. Golovkina (1733–1821) was the daughter of Field Marshal A.I. Shuvalov, brother of I.I. Shuvalov, and the masked ball to which she was invited took place in Saint Petersburg at the palace of the third Shuvalov brother, Count Peter Ivanovich. This lavish masquerade with illuminations was held to mark the birth on 20 September of the future Emperor Paul I.

Court Livery

'The splendour of the uniforms, the luxury of their attire, the wealth of their liveries … the spectacle is so magnificent that no other court in the world could begin to compare'.[1]

SUCH was the view of the French ambassador on the full ceremonial dress of the Imperial Russian Court at the beginning of the twentieth century – admiration indeed from one whose country had been an arbiter of world fashion for over 200 years.

There were strict regulations governing the dress of the Tsar's retinue at the Russian court as early as the 1680s. Each group of court personnel had a particular uniform, which was kept in the Tsar's Treasury and given out to be worn at ambassadorial receptions and formal occasions. Having astonished Versailles in 1718 with the modesty of his attire, which inspired a fashion in Paris for 'dressing like the Tsar', Peter the Great made it his mission on becoming Emperor to impress the whole of Europe with the magnificence of his court. Full court dress made its first appearance at the coronation in 1724, when 100 court servants were given an expensive Western European dress made from imported velvet and the latest fashionable French silk. Later, the lavish dress of the Imperial servants contrasted starkly with the relatively modest attire of the Emperors themselves. In the nineteenth century, this formal eighteenth-century aristocratic attire was adapted into the official uniform for court footmen.

A century after Peter the Great's political reforms, uniforms for court officials were introduced in Russia in order to identify those in State service. Up until then, the robes of the six Russian military orders fulfilled this function. When founding the first of these orders, the Order of Saint Andrew, at the end of the seventeenth century, Peter the Great took inspiration from the traditions of military orders established by other European sovereigns to advance specific political objectives. He developed a

particular interest in the status and traditions of the Order of the Garter, founded in 1348 by King Edward III, following a visit to Windsor Castle and its chapel on Saint George's Day in 1698, where he witnessed Knights of the Order being initiated.

The process of determining the colour and design of a ritual costume for the Knights of the Order of Saint Andrew began in 1720[2] and was finalized with the accession of Empress Anna Ivanovna, who was determined that her court should be the equal of any other European court in its splendour and magnificence. She intended the robes of the orders to play a significant role in realizing this extremely expensive ambition. Any further changes or additions to the robes had to be either initiated or approved by the ruling monarch. The accession of Catherine the Great was the most important milestone in the evolution of the robes of the orders. Whereas previously knights had only worn their robes for each order's individual annual holiday, from 1762 to 1776 they were the main form of court uniform and considered obligatory attire for knights and ladies on high ceremonial days when the Empress wore her crown and Imperial mantle. Wearing the robes of one of the orders was a public demonstration of special services rendered by a knight to the Empire and its ruling monarch. It both increased his social status and strengthened his position at court.

The Emperor Paul I reformed the Imperial system of orders, seeking to make it more closely resemble the chivalric ideal, in which strict Christian piety and norms of behaviour would combine with absolute hierarchical obedience to the Emperor. Under Paul, the robes were standardized and again began to predominate at court, although this did not last long. He was after all attempting to resurrect and consolidate the traditions of ancient knights' orders in Russia at a time when the age of chivalry in Europe was already over. As contemporary witnesses at court events testified,

Emperor Paul's excessive fondness for receptions had unfortunate consequences during the reign of his son. Emperor Alexander was as shocked as everyone else by the immoderation shown by his father in this respect, and the mockery and complaints made a deep impression on him. When he took the throne, he threw himself to the opposite extreme and provoked society's discontent by endeavouring to eliminate all receptions and celebrations.[3]

During his reign, the holidays of most of the orders were cancelled and all robes were abolished. The robes of the officials of the orders were kept not in their personal wardrobes but in the wardrobe of the Chapter of Russian Orders. As a result, in the nineteenth century, they were considered relics and in 1917 they were transferred to the Armoury, where they are kept to this day.

At the very beginning of the reign of Emperor Alexander I, the robes were replaced by a court uniform that became compulsory attire for all public ceremonies. It acted as a marker of the hierarchy of officials, duties and ranks. Each uniform was distinguished by its cut, colour and trimmings, which were dictated by government decree. Even slight alterations to the uniforms had to be sanctioned by the Emperor and were often made on his initiative and sometimes even based on his designs. In 1855, the first official 'Rules on the Wearing by Court Officials of the Prescribed Form of Dress' established five types of uniform – formal, festive, standard, everyday and travelling. It stipulated the days and occasions when each of these types should be worn. Apart from identifying court officials, the uniforms also lent elegance and splendour to court ceremonies, the main purpose of which was to demonstrate the political prestige of the Empire and ruling dynasty.

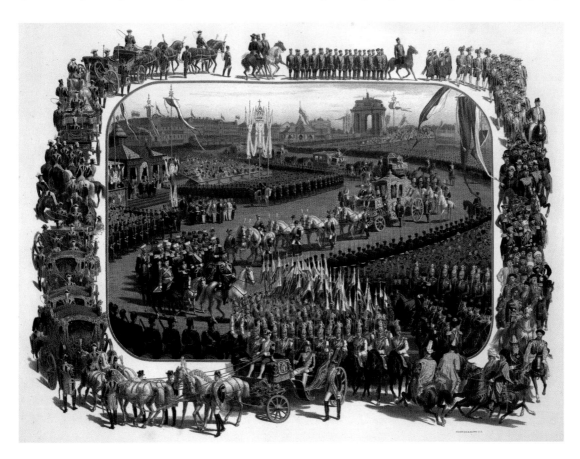

Ceremonial arrival in Moscow for a coronation.
From the book 'Opisanie koronatsii imperatora Aleksandra III i imperatritsy Marii Feodorovny' (Saint Petersburg, 1885).

CLOAK, HAT AND STAFF OF OFFICE OF CHIEF MASTER OF CEREMONIES, 1797

Saint Petersburg
TAILOR – JOHAN KOLB
HAT-MAKER – FEDOT VONCHAKOV
GOLDSMITH – PIERRE TEREMIN
TK-1682, TK-1573, DK-1539/1

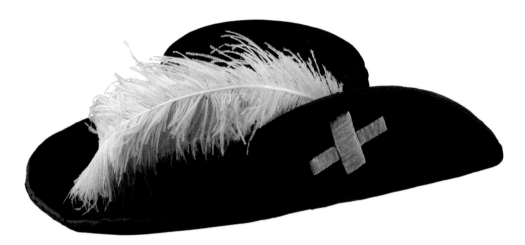

THESE items belong to the robes of one of the highest officials of the military orders – the Chief Master of Ceremonies, who was responsible for overseeing all of the order's festivities and ceremonies. Orders comprised companies of individuals who became members either by birthright or in recognition of a particular service to the monarch. The establishment of such orders in Russia led to the introduction of knights' days, which brought together all members of the order and emphasized their fellowship before State and Church. The court celebrations of the Russian orders were similar to those of European orders: each Russian order celebrated its annual holiday at court on its saint's feast day. The festivities traditionally consisted of a solemn procession to the court's church or order's temple in the capital, a thanksgiving service, the initiation of new members, congratulations of the audience, a formal lunch, supper and ball.

A particular form of dress for representatives of the administration was introduced at the Imperial Court in 1797. The robes of officials and those of knights differed only in the details, which made it possible to determine precisely the status of their wearer in the order's hierarchy. For example, officials did not wear the star of the order on their cloaks. The Chief Master of Ceremonies wore the cloak of the order whose holiday was being celebrated on top of his cloth of silver tabard, which had a gold cross on the front. He wore a hat of black velvet with a light-blue ribbon of the Order of

Saint Andrew sewn onto the brim, and he carried a staff of office made of ebony. There were four interchangeable ivory knobs that screwed onto the top of this staff, each of which bore the star of one of the orders: the Order of Saint Andrew (which is illustrated here), the Order of Saint Catherine, the Order of Saint Alexander Nevsky or the Order of Saint Anna.

This outfit was made for Chief Master of Court Ceremonies P.S. Valuev, who was appointed on 11 April 1797 by Imperial decree.

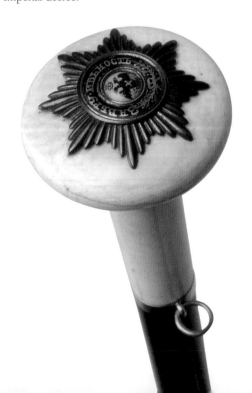

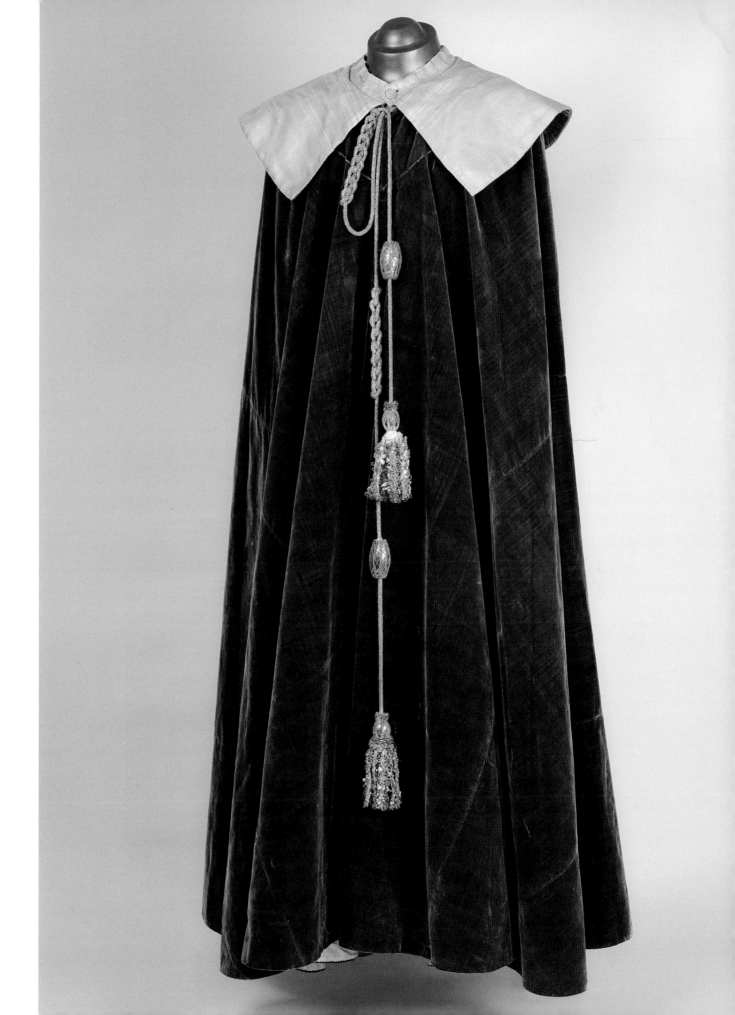

TABARD, BOOTS AND GLOVES BELONGING TO A HERALD OF THE ORDER OF SAINT ANDREW, 1797

Saint Petersburg

TAILOR – JOHAN KOLB
BOOTMAKER – JOHAN DANIEL ERMSCHER
GLOVEMAKER – JOHAN CONRAD WEBER
GOLDSMITH – GERMAN FRIEDRICH POMO
TK-1658, TK-1693/1-2, TK-256/1-2

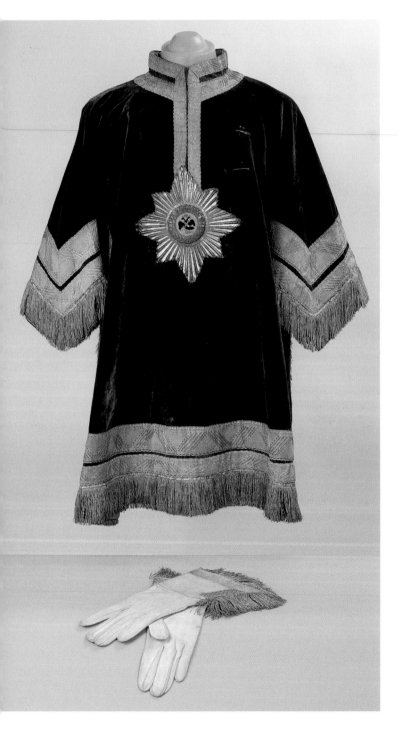

THE Order of Saint Andrew, having been founded by Peter the Great at the very end of the seventeenth century, was the oldest and highest Russian Imperial order; like the other orders, it had two heralds. This ensemble belonged to one of them. The livery played a key role in the orders' ceremonies. The garments were only worn at court and on high ceremonial days. They were made of plain silk velvet embroidered with gold and silver instead of the simple wool of the garments of ancient monastic orders on which they were based.

The annual holiday of the Order of Saint Andrew was celebrated on 30 November. As the order's officials, the heralds took part in this ceremony and also played the role of representatives and messengers. Their costumes were created on the instruction of Emperor Paul I, their colour being that assigned to the order, and the style on traditions established in Western Europe in the Middle Ages.

The tabard, made from green silk velvet with silver braid and fringe and decorated with large stars of the order bearing the motto 'For truth and loyalty', was worn over a wide coat and long narrow breeches of cloth of silver. The herald's livery was complemented by a black velvet hat, trimmed around the brim with braid and a white plume, and with red and white feathers that stood upright, black velvet boots with rosettes and white elkskin gloves trimmed with silver braid and a fringe. The herald held a silver baton with a gold top in the form of the insignia of the order picked out in coloured enamel.

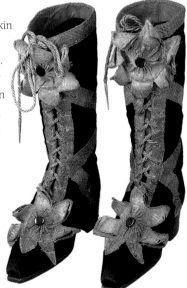

TABARD AND HAT BELONGING TO A HERALD OF THE ORDER OF SAINT CATHERINE, 1797

Saint Petersburg
TAILOR – JOHAN KOLB
HAT-MAKER – FEDOT VONCHAKOV
EMBROIDERER – MARIA ÖSTERREICH
TK-1663, TK-1566

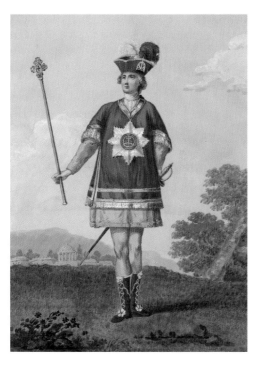

Herald of the Order of Saint Catherine. Watercolour.
From the manuscript book 'Ustanovlenie ob ordenakh'
(Saint Petersburg, 1797), Moscow Kremlin Museums.

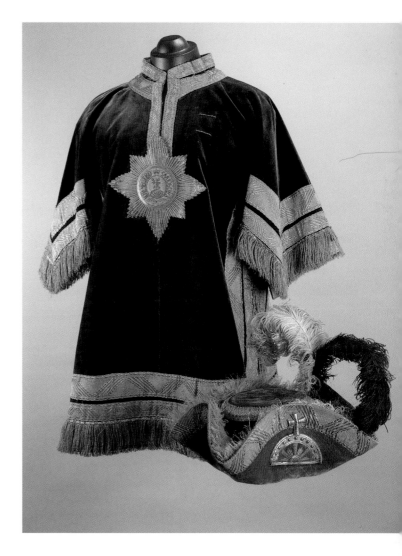

THE Order of Saint Catherine the Great Martyr, founded in 1714 and headed by the Empress, became the second order in European history exclusively for women. Until the middle of the eighteenth century its membership was fairly limited, which may explain the fact that the annual holiday – 24 November – was celebrated at court only from 1742. Ceremonial livery for the order in green, white and gold was introduced the following year. These same colours were subsequently used to create garments for the order's officials, including this outfit, which was made for one of the heralds.

In addition to the green velvet tabard with gold fringe and the hat, trimmed with braid and a plume of ostrich feathers, the livery included a coat and breeches made of pale yellow satin, green velvet boots with braid and rosettes and white elkskin gloves trimmed with a fringe. Large stars of the order and decorative half-wheels on the hat (to commemorate Saint Catherine's martyrdom on the wheel) were made from sequins and silver thread by the specialist embroiderer Maria Österreich. On the stars, the motto of the order encircling the central medallion reads: 'For Love and the Fatherland'.

TABARD BELONGING TO A HERALD OF THE ORDER OF SAINT ALEXANDER NEVSKY, 1797

Saint Petersburg
TAILOR – JOHAN KOLB
GOLD EMBROIDERY – MARIA ÖSTERREICH
TK-1647

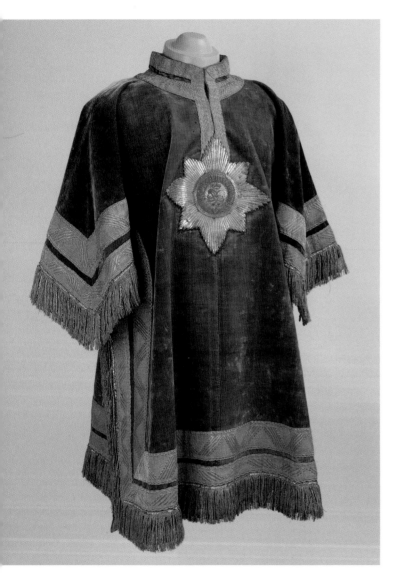

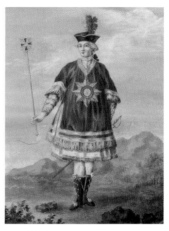

Herald of the Order of
Saint Alexander Nevsky.
Watercolour.
*From the manuscript book
'Ustanovlenie ob ordenakh…'
(Saint Petersburg, 1797), Moscow
Kremlin Museums.*

THE annual holiday of the Order of Saint Alexander Nevsky, considered to be the patron saint of the Imperial capital Saint Petersburg, 'was always celebrated very grandly at court on 30 August, because on that same day the victorious Treaty of Nystad was signed with Sweden.'[4] Peter the Great had conceived this order but Catherine I officially founded it, its official holiday being first recorded in a ceremonial journal in 1728. Nine years later, the order received special knights' robes in white, crimson and silver; these same colours were used at the end of the eighteenth century to make livery for the order's heralds.

This red velvet tabard lined with white silk and trimmed with silver braid and fringing was made for one of the two heralds of the order, either Perepechin or Kazarinov. Both men were advisers on the management of the State Assignat Bank and had been appointed heralds on 11 April 1797 by decree of Emperor Paul I. Both the front and back of the tabard are decorated with stars of the order, embroidered with sequins, silver thread and silk and bearing the motto of the order: 'For Labour and the Fatherland'. The herald's livery also includes a white satin shirt with silver braid; two pairs of breeches, satin for summer and white wool for winter; black velvet boots with silver braid; a black velvet hat with a cross made from ribbon of the order, a white plume, and red and white plumes that stood upright; and gloves with silver braid and a fringe.

TABARD BELONGING TO A HERALD OF THE ORDER OF SAINT ANNA, 1797

Saint Petersburg
TAILOR – JOHAN KOLB
GOLD EMBROIDERY – MARIA ÖSTERREICH
TK-1653

IN some instances, when the heads of European orders moved to other countries their orders were transferred with them as dynastic property. Such was the fate of the Order of Saint Anna, founded in 1735 in Holstein by Karl Friedrich, Duke of Holstein-Gottorp, in memory of his late wife Anna, daughter of Peter the Great. When the Duke's son (the future Peter III) came to Russia in 1742 and was proclaimed heir to the throne, Russian subjects began to be awarded the Order of Saint Anna. The order's annual holiday was celebrated at court on 3 February.

Special robes for the Knights of the Order of Saint Anna are first mentioned in a document of 1746. It refers to them as 'the usual dress of that order', presumably because the livery had already been introduced in Holstein. With the death of Peter III the role of head of the order passed to his son, the future Paul I, who officially added the Order of Saint Anna to the system of Russian court orders and introduced new red, white and gold robes for its knights.

By order of the new Emperor, adviser Ozerov and collegiate assessor Molchanov were appointed heralds of the Order of Saint Anna. Livery corresponding to their duties was made for them in the colours of the order, including this tabard. Work on the heralds' outfits began in June and was completed in November 1797. Fabrics were supplied by the Saint Petersburg merchants M. Shatikhin and P. Sutugin, and the braiding and fringe were supplied by P. Likhachev. The livery comprised a red velvet tabard with gilt braid, fringe and stars of the order bearing the Latin motto 'AMANTIBUS JUSTITIAM, PIETATUM, FIDEM' (To those who love justice, piety and fidelity), a pale yellow satin shirt and breeches, red velvet boots and hat and white gloves with a fringe. The hat was decorated with a white plume, and the cross of the order was stitched onto the upturned brim.

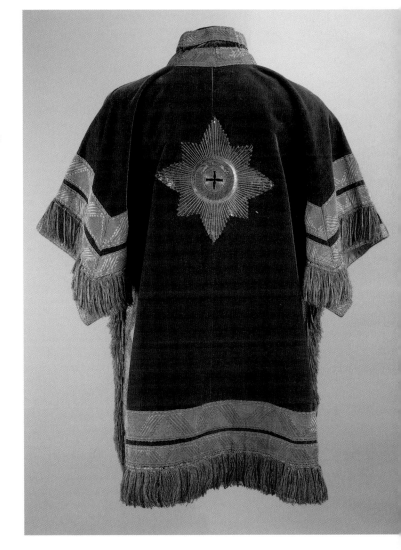

TUNIC (*SUPERVEST*) OF A KNIGHT OF THE ORDER OF SAINT GEORGE, 1798

Saint Petersburg
TK-298

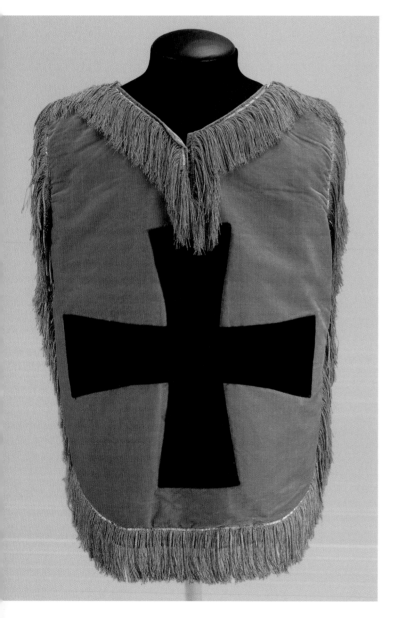

A NUMBER of orders in Europe were dedicated to Saint George, who was considered the protector of warriors. Usually, acceptance into the order was an incentive to future military service, but the Russian Order of Saint George the Grand Martyr and Triumphant, founded in 1769 by Catherine the Great, became the first to admit members for prior honours in battle. In keeping with the exclusively martial character of the order, its knights did not receive any particular robes but were expected to attend the annual holiday on 14 April in military uniform. Emperor Paul I added to their uniform short vests trimmed with gilt fringe in the colour of the sash of the order – orange velvet with a black cross on the front and back.

In 1798, a sample garment made by the Saint Petersburg merchant M. Shatikhin was approved by the Emperor. It was used to make 60 tunics for the Knights of the Order. Some 35 of those that have survived are preserved in the Armoury collection. The hierarchy of the Russian orders underwent an unofficial change in the nineteenth century, which effectively increased the importance of the holiday of the Order of Saint George. It was celebrated at court right up to the end of the monarchy, and the Emperor attended it every year in military uniform. Tunics like this one were worn by Knights of the Order only in 1798 and were abolished after the accession of Alexander I.

FULL COURT DRESS COAT OF CHAMBERLAIN, SECOND HALF OF 19TH CENTURY

Russia
TK-3041, TK-1933, TK-3045

ONE of the highest court ranks at the Imperial Court was that of chamberlain. The chamberlain's duties included daily attendance on the Empress and each member of the Imperial family in turn and the presentation of male visitors. In the eighteenth century, the title of chamberlain was bestowed upon only a handful of individuals, who enjoyed exclusive privileges because of their status. By the nineteenth century, only a fraction of those appointed actually performed any duties and for most it was an honorary award for various kinds of service, which conferred the right to be received at court and to participate in court ceremonies.

From the first third of the eighteenth century, chamberlains were distinguished by the key most graciously bestowed upon them. The decorative key was carried on the left pocket flap, on a light-blue watered silk ribbon tied in a bow. It symbolized the right of the chamberlain to enter the Emperor's private apartments unannounced.

Although the first reference to a special chamberlain's uniform dates to 1801, this particular style dates from about 50 years later. The single-breasted coat is cut from black wool manufactured in Russia and is distinguished by its stiffened, high standing collar and red wool cuffs. It has a hidden fastening, and the gilded heraldic buttons are purely decorative. The use of fake brandenburgs (vertical bands of braid originally used as an opening) in the pattern of the lavish embroidery was regulated by law. The abundance of gold embroidery made these uniforms very expensive for the chamberlains, who had to pay for them themselves. For the most formal ceremonies, the full dress uniform included white trousers with gold stripes down the outer seam and a bicorn hat of black felt trimmed with a plume of white ostrich feathers and gold embroidery matching that on the coat.

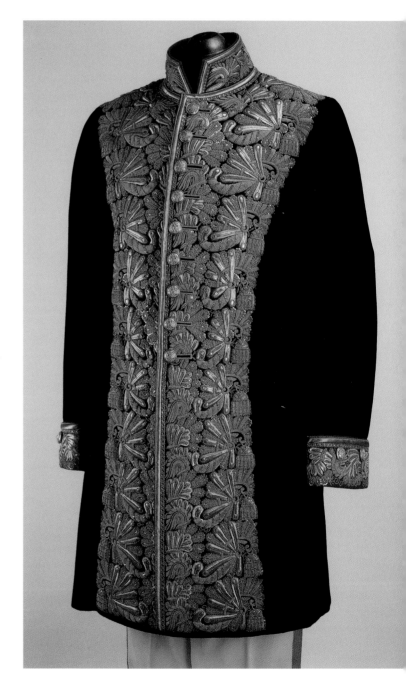

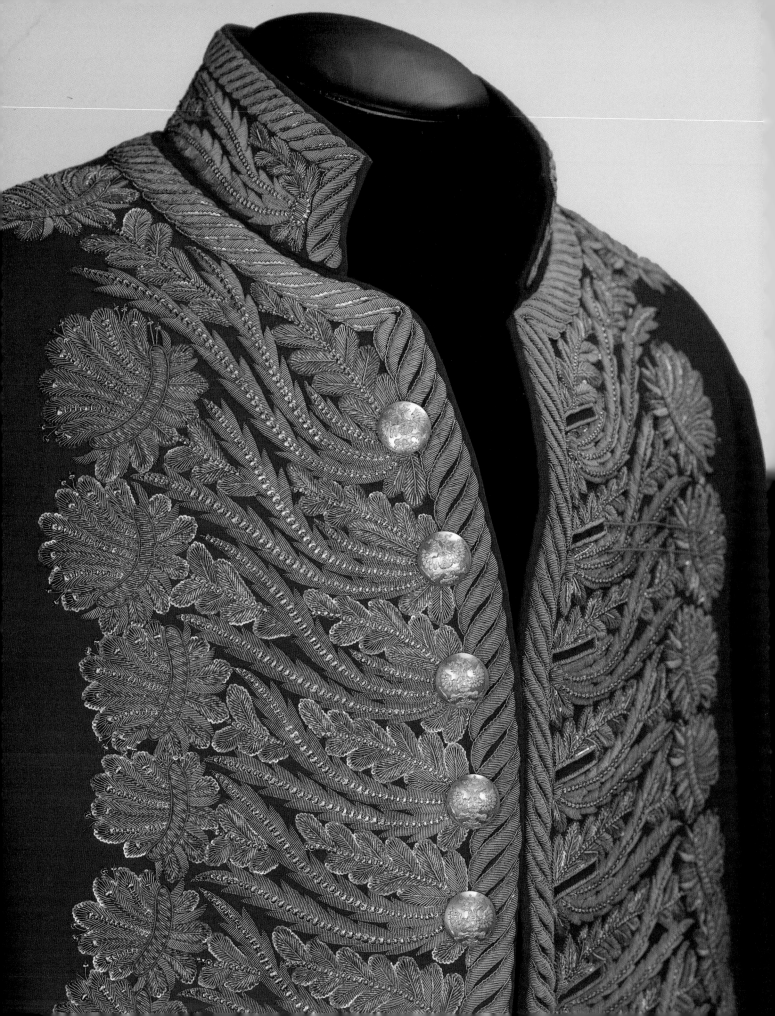

MASTER OF IMPERIAL HOUSEHOLD'S DRESS COAT, SECOND HALF OF 19TH CENTURY

Russia

TK-3042

THIS red wool coat with luxurious gold embroidery and heraldic buttons was part of the full dress uniform of the *kamer-fur'er*, a rank that was introduced into the Imperial Court in the 1730s during the reign of Empress Anna Ivanovna (ruled 1730–40). The duties of the *kamer-fur'er* included the management of court staff and the compilation of special journals, which provide a detailed chronicle of official ceremonies. These journals were used to record all receptions held, outings made and events attended by the Emperor and Empress. In a number of cases the entries include a detailed description of dress. In the nineteenth century, three copies of the journal were made: 'one was laid every morning on the Emperor's writing desk in a sealed envelope; the second, also sealed, was sent to the Minister of the Imperial Court; the third was kept by the *kamer-fur'er* in a special metal box. They were considered highly secret.'[5]

The cut of this full dress uniform was based on the cut of French men's fashionable dress of the second half of the eighteenth century. It consisted of a red wool coat with cut away skirts, a white wool waistcoat trimmed with braid, white wool breeches, white silk stockings, black shoes with buckles and a hat. At the end of the nineteenth and the beginning of the twentieth century, there were three *kamer-fur'ers* on the staff of the Imperial Court: the most senior was M.M. Mikhailov, and his juniors were N.A. Bakhtin and A.E. Stepanov. The senior *kamer-fur'er*, dressed in livery, was present at every official ceremony and grand outing and on some occasions participated actively in such events. On 3 April 1896, during preparations for the coronation of Emperor Nicholas II and Empress Alexandra Feodorovna, he led the procession of court officials bearing the Imperial Regalia from the Winter Palace in Saint Petersburg to the Nikolaevsky Station for their transport onward to Moscow.

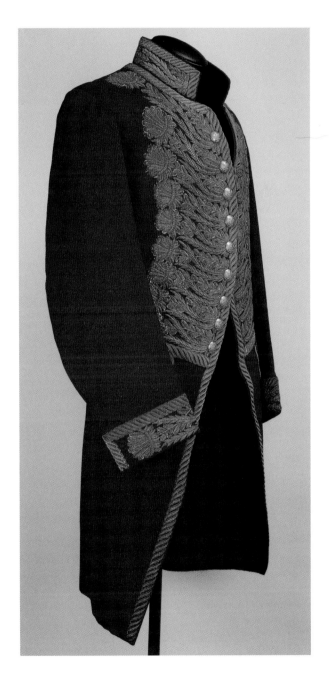

AS well as making processions in their palaces, the Imperial family made them with full equipage (horses and carriages) to the Cathedral of the Transfiguration (Preobrazhensky Cathedral) on 6 August, the day of the Lord's Transfiguration; to the Alexander Nevsky Monastery on 30 August, the annual holiday of the Order of Saint Alexander Nevsky; and to meet brides marrying into the Imperial family, to consecrate churches and to review troops and attend celebrations of military holidays in the capital. The arrangements for such splendid outings were managed by the office specifically responsible for the court carriages and stables, which was reorganized in 1786 into the Court Stable Bureau and in 1891 into the Court Stable Department.

Particular attention during these outings was devoted by the Ministry of the Imperial Court to the liveries of the court coachmen and the postilions, who rode the near horse of the harnessed lead pair. Sample garments approved by the Emperor were used to make individual uniforms for each of the postilions and were cut to fit the torso closely; these uniforms were kept in the Livery Depository of the Winter Palace. Examples of coachmen's garments and several luxurious postilions' jackets that were no longer used were given to the museum of the Court Stable Department at the end of the nineteenth century and passed on to the Armoury at the beginning of the twentieth century. A number of distinguishing features indicate that these postilions' jackets date from the reign of Emperor Nicholas I.

The green and light-blue velvet jacket (far right) with epaulettes is decorated with gilt braid, cord, tassels and fringe and five rows of heraldic buttons. A metal shield bearing the lesser coat of arms of Empress Alexandra Feodorovna, the wife of Nicholas I, is sewn onto a green band on the left sleeve. This coat of arms is made up of two elements – the double-headed Russian eagle and the single-headed Prussian eagle bearing the initials FWR (Friedrich Wilhelm Rex). Friedrich Wilhelm III of Prussia was Alexandra Feodorovna's

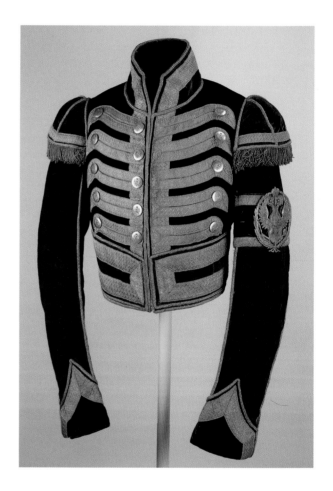

father. The name of the postilion for whom the jacket was made is written on the lining – A. Stepanov.

The second jacket (above) is made from dark-blue wool trimmed with crimson and green velvet and is decorated more modestly. Three rows of flat gilt buttons bear the coat of arms of the Kingdom of Poland, which became part of the Russian Empire in 1815 as a result of the Congress of Vienna. They indicate that the postilion's jacket was probably made for one of Emperor Nicholas I's visits to Warsaw, where he was crowned King of Poland on 12 May 1829.

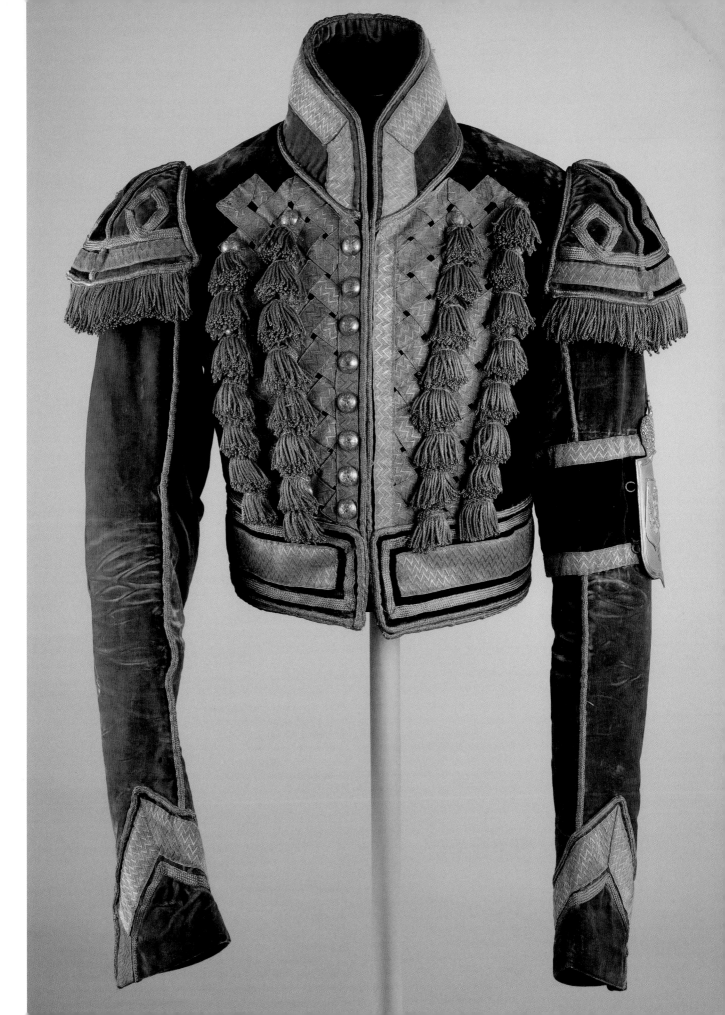

COACHMEN'S JACKETS, 1881–1917

Russia
тк-1876, тк-3046

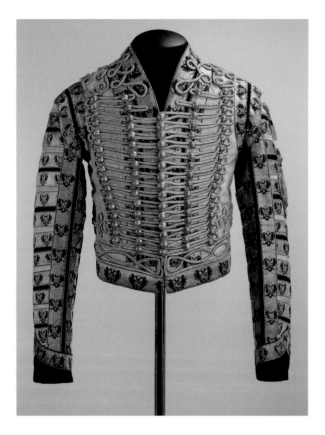

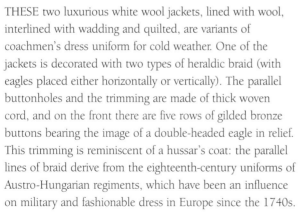

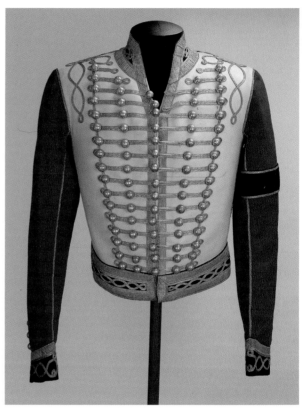

THESE two luxurious white wool jackets, lined with wool, interlined with wadding and quilted, are variants of coachmen's dress uniform for cold weather. One of the jackets is decorated with two types of heraldic braid (with eagles placed either horizontally or vertically). The parallel buttonholes and the trimming are made of thick woven cord, and on the front there are five rows of gilded bronze buttons bearing the image of a double-headed eagle in relief. This trimming is reminiscent of a hussar's coat: the parallel lines of braid derive from the eighteenth-century uniforms of Austro-Hungarian regiments, which have been an influence on military and fashionable dress in Europe since the 1740s.

The name of the owner of the jacket is written on the lining in Roman letters – 'Smith', suggesting that an Englishman was employed at court.

The second jacket, which according to an inscription on the lining was meant 'for rain', has red wool sleeves and black velvet collar, belt, cuffs and sleeve bands. The jacket fastens with hooks. The 81 heraldic buttons and trimming of gilt braid are purely decorative, as are the figures on the belt, cuffs, shoulders and collar. The paper label sewn into the lining bears the name of the owner of the jacket – 'court coachman Sukhoruchenko'. There is also a stamp indicating that the jacket belonged to the wardrobe of the Court Stable.

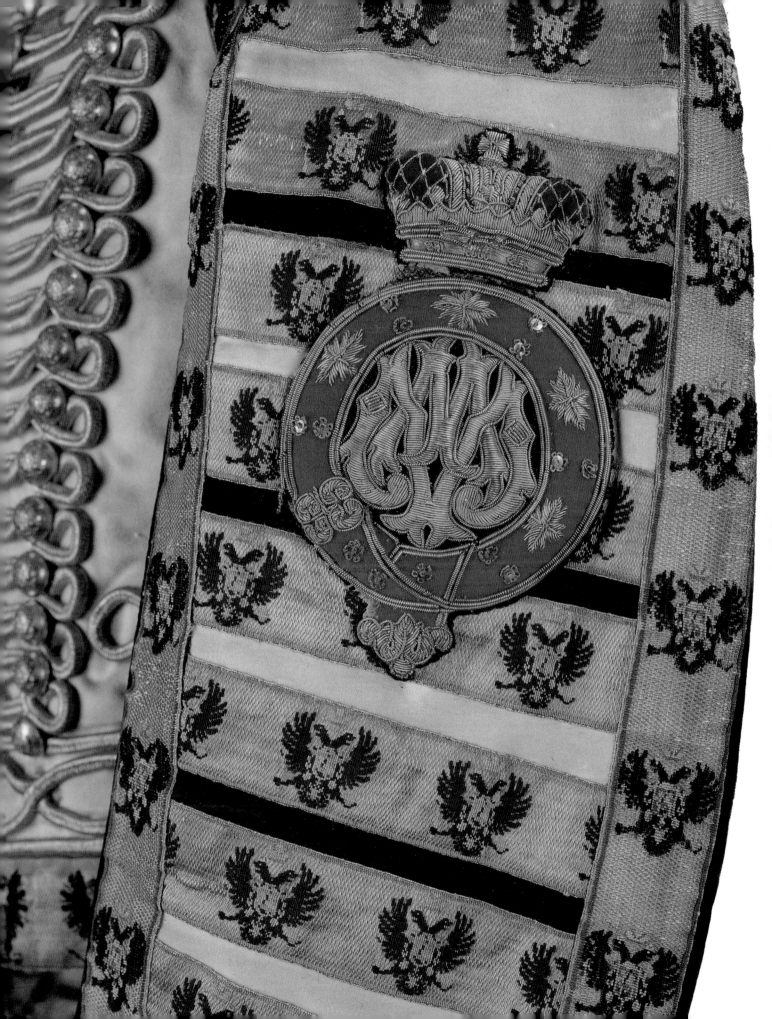

POSTILION'S JACKET AND CAP, 1881–1917

Russia

CAP – SAINT PETERSBURG, FABRIQUE DE CHAPEAUX BRUNO *FRÈRES*

TK-3051, TK-1590

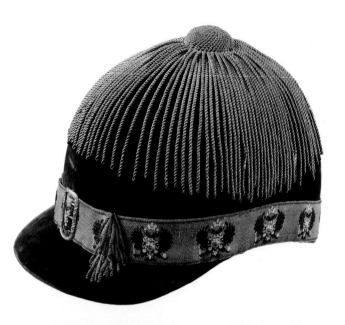

THE variety of coachmen's and postilions' jackets preserved in the Armoury reveals the strict regulation of their attire in accordance not only with the importance of the Imperial outing but also with the season. Most of the jackets are embroidered with the monogram of the Empress Maria Feodorovna, which dates them to the reigns of Alexander III and Nicholas II.

This jacket of fine black wool is trimmed with heraldic braid, which is edged with ornamental gilt cord. The ornamental appliqué on the back and round the lower front is made from the same cord. The jacket is decorated with 66 gilded heraldic buttons arranged in rows, which gradually increase in size. On the right sleeve is a badge of red wool and red velvet with the monogram of Empress Maria Feodorovna embroidered in gilt thread. The monogram is composed of the letters MF beneath the Imperial crown and is enclosed within a circle resembling a twisted strap, which represents an element of horse tack.

The peaked cap that matches this jacket is made of black velvet; the top of its crown is decorated with a button and a gilt fringe, and there is a band of heraldic braid fastened with a metal buckle round the lower edge. The black silk lining is quilted with wadding and bears the gold dye stamp of the famous St Petersburg hat-making workshop, Bruno *frères*. Fournⁿˢ DE S.A.I./LE Grand Duc Heritier A.A.. This business was based at No. 36 Nevsky Prospekt, one of the most important streets for shopping for fashion in late nineteenth- and early twentieth-century Saint Petersburg.

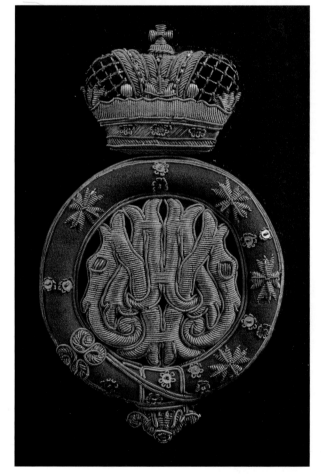

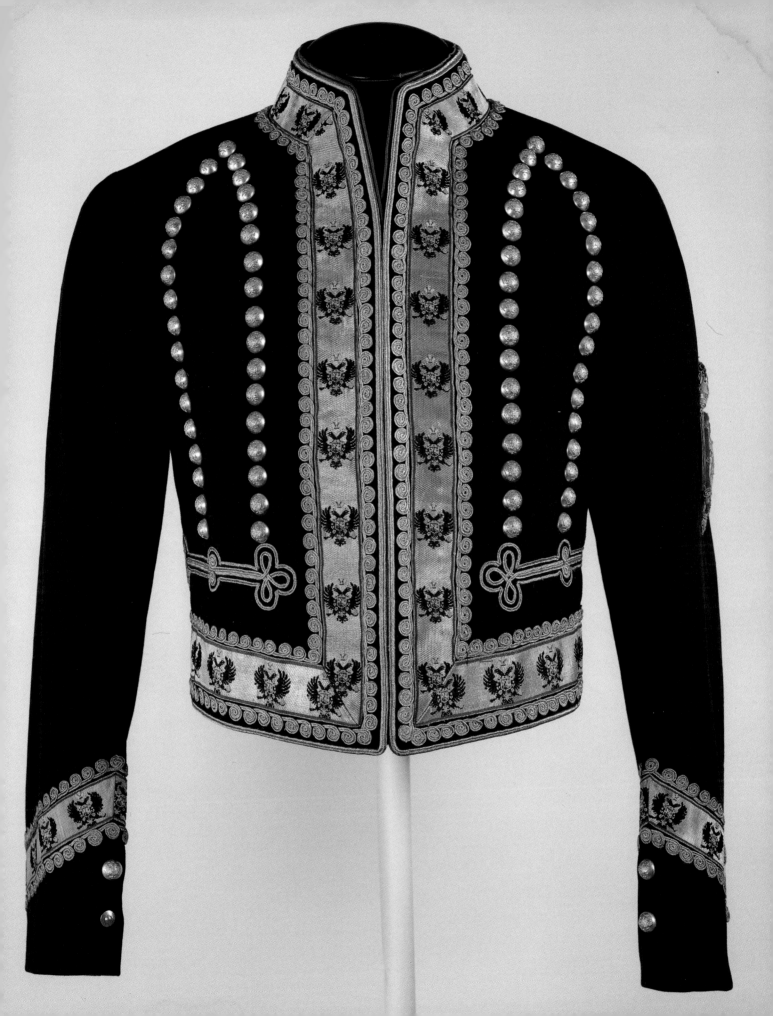

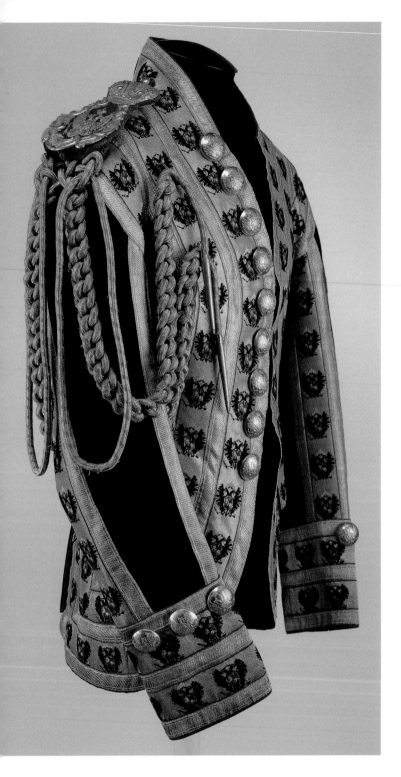

COACHMAN'S LIVERY COAT, 1883–1917

Russia
TK-3050

THIS livery coat was part of the dress attire of the court coachman. It is made from black wool lined with red cashmere and is decorated round the edges with bands of wide braid woven with heraldic double-headed eagles in black and red silk on a gold background, on the front opening and round the cuffs with 23 large gilt heraldic buttons, and on the right shoulder with an aiguillette of gold cord and a metal epaulette imprinted with the image of a double-headed eagle within a cartouche beneath a crown. There is a badge of red wool on the left sleeve; the monogram that was originally sewn onto this badge is missing.

Similar dress liveries, differing slightly in the details of the cut and trimming, were given to a number of court servants, including footmen. This coachman's livery was made for particularly important Imperial ceremonial outings, primarily those relating in some way to coronation celebrations. When Nicholas II arrived in Moscow for his coronation, the ceremonial procession was led by a squadron of horse-guardsmen, followed by the Tsar riding a white horse. Empress Alexandra Feodorovna and the Dowager Empress Maria Feodorovna followed in antique gold coaches that had been borrowed from the Armoury for the occasion. The carriages were driven by coachmen dressed in liveries identical to this one, which was transferred to the museum at the beginning of the twentieth century from the Livery Depository of the Winter Palace.

COACHMAN'S JACKET, 1881–1917

Russia

TK-3054

THIS jacket of dark-blue wool trimmed with narrow gilt braid appears to have been part of the coachman's everyday uniform and was probably made for cold weather. The front is decorated with 94 plain gilded buttons, and there is a badge on the right sleeve bearing the monogram of Empress Maria Feodorovna. The lining is inscribed with the Russian first name 'Zachar'. The museum collection contains another jacket with the same inscription that is made of green velvet with heraldic buttons and was clearly the dress variant of the uniform.

The full dress livery of coachmen consisted of a single-breasted jacket with the cut of the back similar to that of a tailcoat, but without the tails. It was decorated with rows of small buttons and worn with a round peaked cap, white breeches, jockey boots with spurs and white chamois leather gloves with gauntlets.

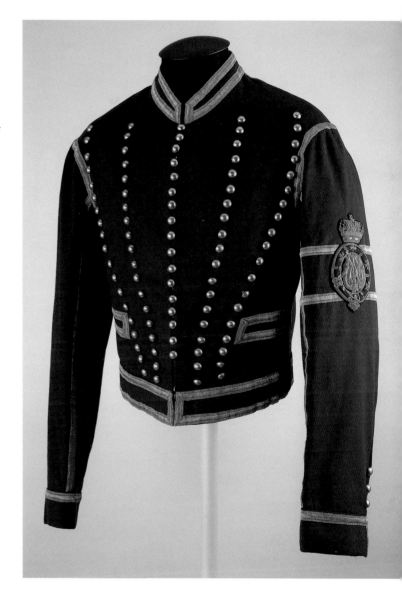

Fancy Dress

By order of Their Imperial Majesties, the Chief Marshal of the Imperial Court has the honour of informing you of your invitation on Tuesday 11 February, at 8.30 in the evening, to a spectacle at the Imperial Hermitage. Ladies and gentlemen to come in costumes from the time of Tsar Alexey Mikhailovich....[1]

SOME 416 of these invitations were sent out on 1 January 1903 from the Chief Marshal's department to representatives of the Russian aristocracy. The idea of organizing a ball at court in old Russian costumes had come to Empress Alexandra Feodorovna over breakfast on 29 December 1902, as she listened to an argument between Pavel Vasil'evich, the son of the famous poet V.A. Zhukovsky, and Baron V.B. Frederiks, the Minister of the Imperial Court. They were discussing Peter the Great's dress reforms, Frederiks defending the innovations of the great reformer. In response, Zhukovsky maintained that Russian national dress was far more aesthetically pleasing than frock-coats and embroidered court uniforms.[2]

The costume ball was scheduled to coincide with one of the theatrical evenings that usually took place at the Hermitage Theatre in the Winter Palace during the Season.[3] 'No one is capable of talking about anything but the ball in Saint Petersburg,' wrote Count P.S. Sheremet'ev in his diary. 'Everyone is reading Savvaitov, Zabelin and Viskovatov. Tailors and dressmakers are arriving every minute.'[4] Moreover, 'everyone kept their costume a secret, in order to surprise other guests on the night.'[5]

It was generally acknowledged at the time that the most beautiful costumes were made at the workshop of the famous Moscow dressmaker N.P. Lamanova, 'whose talent, taste and style were exceptional. She was a Russian genius of elegance with whom no one could compare, not even the finest fashion houses in France.'[6] From 1898, she was a supplier to the court of Grand Duke Sergey Alexandrovich, and it was apparently in her workshop that the lavish fancy dress costumes worn by Grand Duchess Elizabeth Feodorovna and Grand Duke Sergey Alexandrovich were created. These costumes were based on sketches by the watercolour artist S.S. Solomko and were richly embroidered by nuns in Moscow's convents under the supervision of and assisted by M.N. Ermolova, maid of honour to Their Imperial Majesties.

Several of those invited ordered their costumes from the Brothers A. and L. Leifert in Saint Petersburg, although the vast majority had them made in the workshops of Saint Petersburg's Imperial Theatre wardrobe. Some of the sketches for these costumes were made by the leading theatre artist A.Ya. Golovin, but most members of the Imperial family sought the services of I.A. Vsevolozhsky, director of the Imperial Hermitage and former director of the Imperial Theatres. Contemporary memoirs recall Vsevolozhsky's artistic skills and how he personally made the initial sketches for the theatre costumes, which were usually completed by the artist E.P. Ponomarev.

For the heir to the throne, Grand Duke Mikhail Alexandrovich, I.A. Vsevolozhsky proposed a sketch by E.P. Ponomarev, which he described as 'the outfit worn by Alexey Mikhailovich [Tsar 1645–76] on the day he chose his bride.'[7] The costume was made by the leading wardrobe-master of the Imperial Theatres, the Italian I.I. Caffi, and was deemed the most lavish of all, as it was iridescent with jewelled decorations belonging to the Dowager Empress Maria Feodorovna.

E.P. Ponomarev and I.A. Vsevolozhsky labelled the sketch of the costume for Empress Alexandra Feodorovna 'Tsarina in Grand Attire'. It was based on an ancient icon worshipped by the Imperial family – the 'Exaltation of the Cross' from the Church of the Crucifixion within the Moscow Kremlin – and portrayed the first wife of Tsar Alexey Mikhailovich Romanov, Maria Il'inichna Miloslavskaya. The costume was made by the talented wardrobe-mistress of the Imperial Theatres A.F. Ivashchenko, and the design for the decoration of the dress and headdress made by artists from the firm of Fabergé. On 16 January 1903, A.K. Fabergé and I.A. Vsevolozhsky were invited to the Empress's dressing-room, where they spent two hours selecting jewels from the crown diamonds and the Empress's personal jewellery box. 'They have so many incredible decorations,' wrote I.A. Vsevolozhsky, 'which they

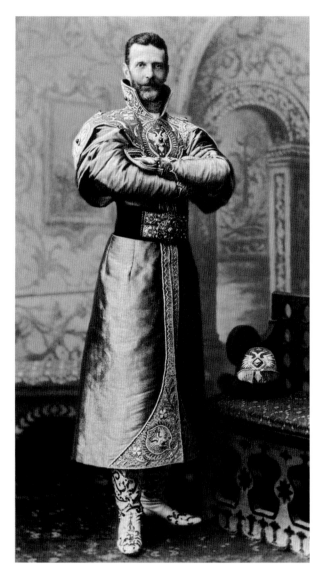

Grand Duke Sergey Alexandrovich.
Photogravure from the photograph by D.Asikritov. 1904.
Scientific Library of Russian Academy of Arts, Saint Petersburg

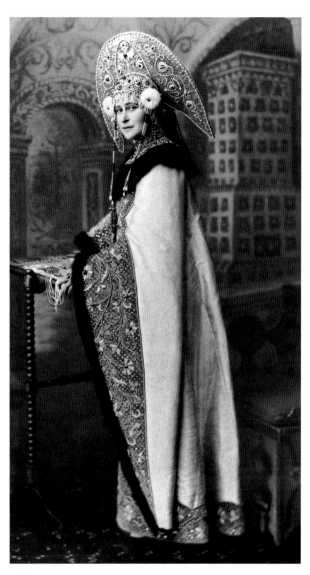

Grand Duchess Elizabeth Feodorovna.
Photogravure from the photography by D.Asikritov. 1904.
Scientific Library of Russian Academy of Ars, Saint Petersburg

never show to anyone'.[8] The front of the costume was adorned with an enormous flat emerald 'as big as the palm of one's hand', framed with little diamonds. Seeing it at the ball for the first time, Grand Duchess Maria Georgievna 'could not refrain from commenting that it was probably through just such an emerald that Nero had watched the Great Fire of Rome.'[9]

The Emperor also 'gave orders to find him an appropriate costume. He wanted something full-length and not too garish,' wrote I.A. Vsevolozhsky, 'but it was the Empress's wish that His Majesty's attire should resemble hers'.[10] The Emperor's appearance in fancy dress, particularly

in front of diplomats, was somewhat controversial. A number of individuals close to the court were critical of his decision, but nobody dared to express such views aloud.

The 'Russian' ball was so exclusive and impressive an event that many remembered it as the last ball in the history of Russia.[11] Much was spoken and written about it throughout 1903, and those who were fortunate enough to be among the guests remembered it for the rest of their lives. 'One was transported several centuries back in time. A truly fairytale impression was created by the profusion of traditional national costumes, richly decorated with rare furs, magnificent diamonds, pearls and semi-precious

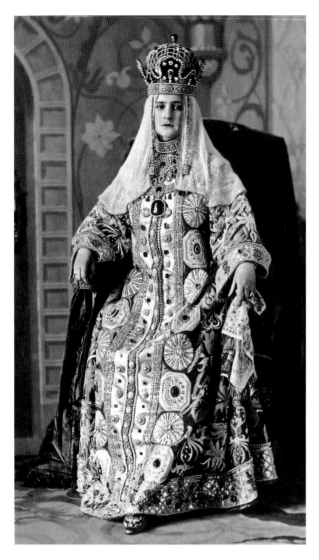

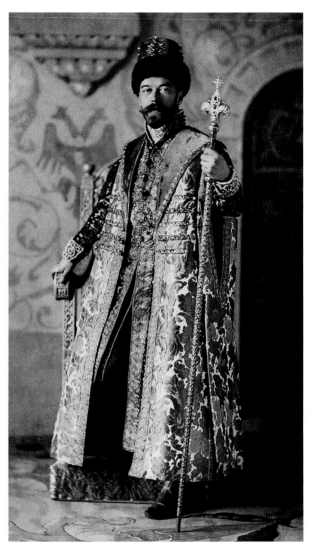

Empress Alexandra Feodorovna.
Photograph by L.S. Levitsky. 1903. Saint Petersburg State Museum of Theatre and Music

Emperor Nicholas II (dressed as Alexey Mikhailovich).
Phototype from the photograph by L.S. Levitsky. Saint Petersburg 1904. Department of Manuscripts, Prints and Graphics of the Moscow Kremlin Museums, arch.60, act.110, fol.1.

stones, most in their original settings. The family jewels were out in an abundance that exceeded all expectations.'[12]

Due to illness, the Dowager Empress Maria Feodorovna and the Grand Duke and Heir were unable to attend the spectacle, so the decision was taken to repeat the festivities especially for them in the Concert Hall of the Winter Palace on 13 February. The same guests were invited, with the addition of the diplomatic corps. Upon arrival at the ball, 'all of the ambassadors were momentarily overwhelmed…. They spent a long time greatly admiring the costumes and making compliments.'[13]

After the event, an album was published containing photographs of the participants of the ball dressed in their historical costumes. I.A. Vsevolozhsky had come up with the idea for this publication and shared it with the Empress over dinner on 11 February, correctly supposing that it would 'be an imperishable memento of a truly magnificent party.'[14]

Many of the costumes from the court balls of February 1903, including that worn by the Empress, have survived to this day and are currently preserved in the collection of the State Hermitage Museum in Saint Petersburg, although the jewels have long since been removed. The only costume to have been preserved in its original state – with all its decorations intact – is that of Emperor Nicholas II, who gave it to the Armoury during an Imperial visit to Moscow on 2 April 1903.

FANCY DRESS COSTUME OF EMPEROR NICHOLAS II, 1903

FABRIC – MOSCOW, A. & V. SAPOZHNIKOVY
ROBES, BELT – SAINT PETERSBURG, IMPERIAL THEATRE WARDROBE WORKSHOPS, WARDROBE-MASTER I.I. CAFFI
HAT – SAINT PETERSBURG, FABRIQUE DE CHAPEAUX BRUNO *FRÈRES*
BUTTONS – WESTERN EUROPE, 17TH CENTURY
JEWELS – RUSSIA, SECOND HALF OF 17TH CENTURY; TURKEY, 17TH CENTURY
TK-2921, TK-2922, TK-2923, TK-2924

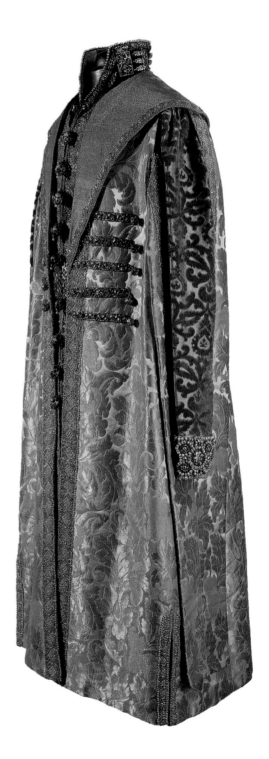

THIS costume was passed to the Armoury because it was decorated with jewels that had been kept in the Kremlin Treasury since the seventeenth century and belonged to the Russian Tsars. The costume is a creative interpretation of the traditional garments of the privileged section of Russian society in the second half of the seventeenth century. This traditional costume was composed of multiple layers, three or four garments being worn one on top of the other in a specific order. They concealed the body entirely, being full-skirted and full-length. Their impressive volume, weight and length rendered the wearer's movement slow and stately.

While the curator of the Armoury, Yu.V. Arsen'ev, transported the jewels to Saint Petersburg for use at the 'Russian' ball, the Moscow firm of Sapozhnikovy supplied the patterned fabrics, immensely complex woven silks that imitated seventeenth-century Italian textiles. At the beginning of the twentieth century, this firm specialized in the manufacture of fabrics such as these, which were distinguished by their exceptional quality and were highly valued not only in Russia but also abroad. Artists working at the firm studied fabrics and designs in museums, archives and private collections, creatively reworking them into new products.

The leading wardrobe-master of the Imperial Theatres, I.I. Caffi, was charged with designing and making the costume for the Emperor; he was assisted by two dressmakers. This costume was called the 'Tsar's Lesser attire', although this name is confusing as the essential outer layer of historic Tsars' dress, both greater and lesser, was the *platno*, a cloak worn with a symbolically decorated shoulder collar (*barmy*), a very different garment from the outer layer of this costume. The fancy dress comprised two long flowing garments: an overgown, referred to in the final wardrobe accounts as a '*shuba*'[15] or fur-lined gown, and an undergown. A number of special features suggests that the *shuba* is, in fact, an *opashen*, a formal summer outer garment very popular at the court of Tsar Alexey Mikhailovich. It did not have a fur lining, but had a turndown collar, slits in the side and bands of jewels

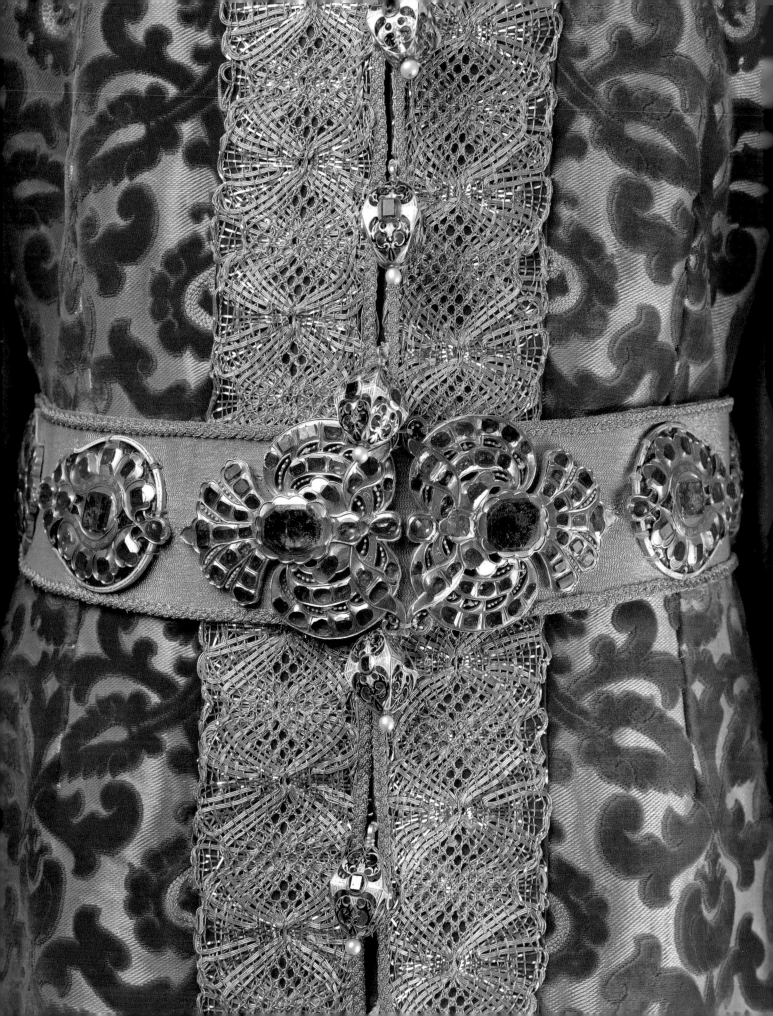

across the front opening. Particularly characteristic are the long hanging sleeves, which in traditional Russian dress served a purely decorative function and either hung to the floor or were folded over one another at the back.

The middle layer of the Emperor's fancy dress costume is a full-length coat (*kaftan*), belted at the waist and with flared skirt. Its sleeves are close-fitting, gathered at the armhole, and they end with a cuff of heavy embroidery. The cut is clearly an improvisation on the part of the wardrobe-master, because sleeves were not cut in this way in seventeenth-century Russian dress. The cuffs originally belonged to Tsar Feodor Ioannovich (ruled 1676–82). They are made of silver brocade with embroidery incorporating large pearls, gold studs and cut diamonds (see p.8). The coat fastens with hooks, over which are stitched large carved gold buttons ornamented with enamel and precious stones. Different shapes and sizes of large, gold Turkish studs, decorated with rubies and emeralds, are stitched to the belt that was worn over the coat round the waist. Two strips of red satin are sewn to the front of the coat, which has a standing-collar known in the seventeenth century as a *kozyr*. This detail was the wardrobe-master's way of deliberately implying the presence of the third obligatory component of the traditional Russian dress – the *zipun*, or inner coat, which wrapped to one side.

The hat for the costume was made by Bruno *frères*, suppliers to the management of the Imperial Theatres. The crown is decorated with gold and enamelled hat jewels inset with pearls and precious stones, in the shape of stylized pomegranate flowers; a band of jewels is attached right round the lower edge of the crown, and a deep sable fur trim.

In addition to the items given to the Armoury, the costume also included plain silk wide trousers, a shirt with an embroidered collar and a belt with tassels. The boots were made of yellow morocco leather lined with silk and trimmed with velvet, and they had silver embossed heels. They had been commissioned from the master bootmaker G.F. Sitnov, supplier to His Imperial Majesty.[16]

During the ball, the Emperor carried a gold staff, decorated with precious stones and enamel, which had been borrowed from the Armoury. Its top was in the shape of a lily crowned with a cross.[17] This staff originally belonged to Tsar Alexey Mikhailovich and was brought to him from Istanbul in 1658. Nicholas II wore this costume on three occasions: 11 and 13 February, and also 3 March

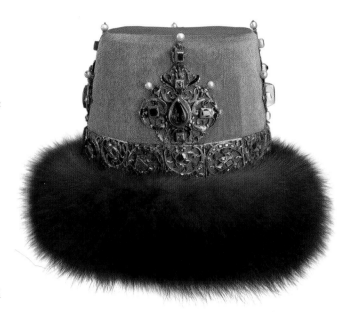

1903, when he posed for a photograph in the Concert Hall of the Winter Palace.

After the costume ball that took place at the Winter Palace on 11 (and 13) February 1903, Empress Alexandra Feodorovna commissioned a series of photographic portraits and group shots of the guests in their fancy dress costumes. These photographs were taken at Saint Petersburg's finest photographic establishments – L.S. Levitsky, Boissonnas & Eggler, Rentz & Schröder – and the photography studios of the Imperial Theatres and others.[18] They served as the basis for the album of phototypes that was published in 1904 by the Department for the Preparation of State Papers. The album contained around 200 images, a veritable costume portrait gallery of the Imperial family and highest society of the Russian Empire at the beginning of the twentieth century.

The photograph of Nicholas II dressed as Tsar Alexey Mikhailovich was taken at the studio of Lev Sergeevich (see p.102). The Levitsky family of photographers had been linked to the Imperial Court for several generations. Sergey L'vovich Levitsky, one of the first Russian photographers, studied the basics of photography in 1840 in Paris under the tutelage of Louis G.M. Daguerre himself before opening his *Svetopis'* studio on Nevsky Prospekt in 1849. In 1877 he was appointed photographer to Their Imperial Majesties. His son Lev Sergeevich Levitsky, who worked with his father for many years, inherited the business after Sergey's death in 1898 and preserved its reputation as one of the finest and most renowned in Russia.

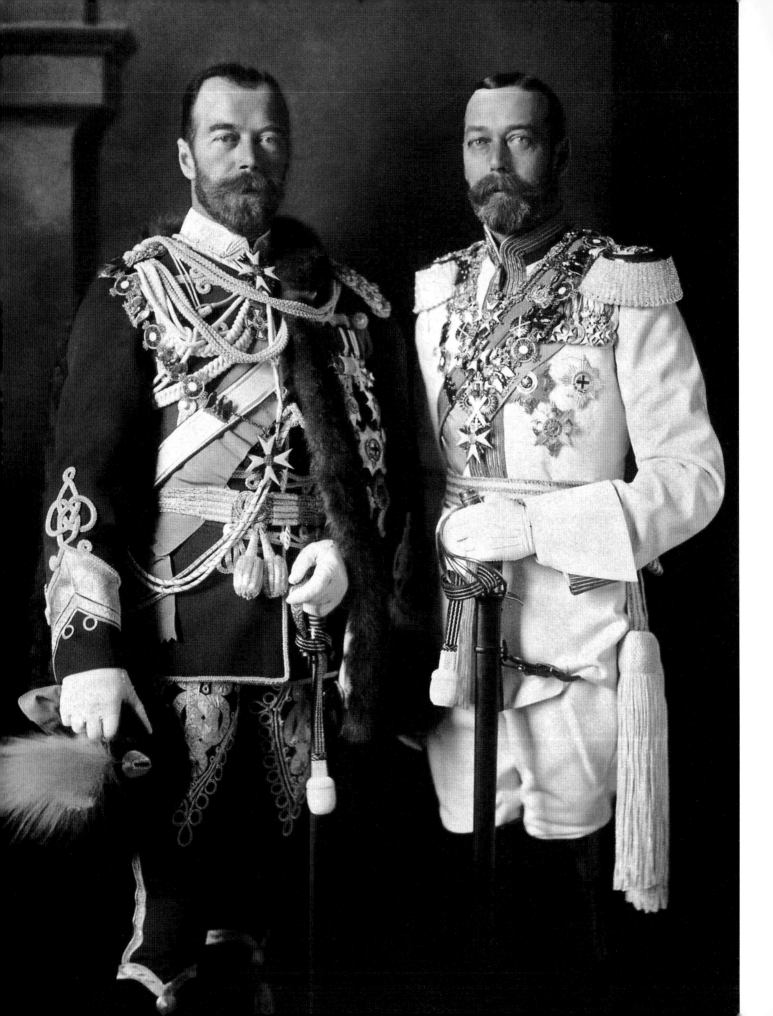

Notes

INTRODUCTION

1. Cracraft, James, *The Petrine Revolution in Russian Imagery* (Chicago, 1997), p.130.
2. Bowlt, John E. (ed.), *Russian Art of the Avant-Garde: Theory and Criticism 1902–1934* (revised and enlarged edition, London, 1988), pp.55–6.
3. Petr Chaadaev, 'Letters on the Philosophy of History', in Marc Raeff (ed.), *Russian Intellectual History: an Anthology* (New Jersey, 1978), p.166.
4. Cracraft (1997), p.138.
5. Hughes, Lindsey, *Russia in the Age of Peter the Great* (New Haven, London, 1998), p.282.

DRESS AS A REFLECTION OF IMPERIAL GRANDEUR

1. From a speech made by the chancellor and president of the College of Foreign Affairs, G.I. Golovkin, during festivities to celebrate the conclusion of the Treaty of Nystad in Saint Petersburg's Trinity Cathedral on 22 October 1721. See *Panegiricheskaya literatura petrovskogo vremeni* (Moscow, 1979), p.298.
2. From the seventeenth century to the beginning of the eighteenth century, all foreigners from Western Europe speaking Romance or Germanic languages were referred to in Russia as 'Germans' (Russian *nemtsy*, from the word *nemoi*, meaning 'dumb' or 'mute'). It was only possible to communicate with them with the help of a translator, whereas this was not the case for the majority of foreigners from Eastern Europe who spoke Slavic languages, which belong to the same family of languages as Russian.
3. Comprehensive research has not yet been carried out into the principles by which foreign words used to designate the component parts and decoration of Western European style dress were adopted into Russian. A number of generally accepted terms came from Germany and France e.g. Russian *shlafrok* from *Schlafrok*, meaning nightgown (contemporary dressing gown); *galstuk* from *Halstuch*, meaning cravat; Russian *kamzol* from French *camisole*, meaning waistcoat; *kyuloty* from *culottes*, meaning breeches; *roba* from *robe*, meaning gown; *glazet* from *glacé*, meaning lustring. A significant number was also drawn from the lexicon of traditional Russian costume (e.g. *shtany* – breeches, *kaftan* – coat, *chulki* – stockings, *bashmaki* – shoes, *porty* – trousers, *sorochka* – shirt).
4. Rossiiskii gosudarstvennyi arkhiv drevnikh aktov (Russian State Archive of Ancient Acts; hereinafter RGADA), arch.1239, inv.3, pt.78, act.34741, fols.323–4.
5. *Dnevnik kamer-yunkera Berkhgol'tsa* (Moscow, 1857–60) vol.4, p.51.

6. 'Rasskaz Berkhgol'tsa o koronatsii Ekaterina I', *Russkii arkhiv* (Moscow, 1883), pt.1, p.372.
7. *Kamer-fur'erskii tseremonial'nyi zhurnal* 1770 g. (Saint Petersburg, 1856), p.229.
8. 'Zapiski Bernulli,' *Russkii arkhiv* (Moscow, 1902), bk.1, p.16. Bernulli alludes to the fact that Catherine the Great, having lost her figure with age, eschewed dress that would accentuate her waist and instead chose to hide her figure under loose-fitting garments. Her wedding dress, which is preserved in the collection of the Moscow Kremlin Museums, has a 48-cm (19-inch) waist.
9. *Kamer-fur'erskii tseremonial'nyi zhurnal* 1775 g. (Saint Petersburg, 1878), p.750.
10. Moy, C. Graf, *Als Diplomat am Zarenhof* (Munich, 1971), p.61.
11. Tyutcheva, A.F., *Pri dvore dvukh imperatorov. Vospominaniya. Dnevnik 1853–1882* (Moscow, 1928–9), vol.1, p.36.

CORONATIONS

1. Notes by A.A. Mosolov, head of the secretariat at the Ministry of the Imperial Court, Gosudarstvennyi arkhiv Rossiiskoi Federatsii (State Archive of Russian Federation; hereafter GARF), arch.1463, inv.1, act.1115, fol.265.
2. From the diary of Grand Duke K.K. Romanov, GARF, arch.660, inv.1, act.4, fol.60 *verso*.
3. From a letter from Empress Maria Feodorovna to her mother Louise of Denmark, GARF, arch.642, inv.1, act.648, letter 20, Moscow, Kremlin, 19/31 May 1883.
4. RGADA, arch.396, inv.2, act.1230, fols.8–8 *verso*.
5. 'Pis'ma o Rossii v Ispaniyu duka de-Liriya, byvshego pervym ispanskim poslannikom v Rossii pri imperatore Petre II i v nachale tsarstvovaniya Anny Ioannovny,' *Osmnadtsatyi vek. Istoricheskii sbornik* (Moscow, 1869), bk.3, p.33.
6. RGADA, arch.1239, inv.3, act.34739, fol.14; act.34740, fols.1, 91.
7. RGADA, arch. 248, inv. 90, act.7465, fols.48, 49.
8. *Vladel'tsy pavlovskogo dvortsa. Pavel Petrovich. Velikii Knyaz'. Imperator* (Saint Petersburg, 2001), p.110.
9. Chartoryiskii, A., *Memuary* (Moscow, 1998), pp.95–6; Leonov, O.G. and Ul'yanov, I.E., *Regulyarnaya pekhota: 1698–1801* (Moscow, 1995), p.157.
10. Rossiiskii gosudarstvennyi istoricheskii arkhiv (Russian State Historical Archive; hereinafter RGIA), arch.469, inv.2, act.1413, fol.597; act.1419, fols.287–287 *verso*.
11. The master gold embroiderer who made the uniform buttonholes for the Emperor during his stay in Moscow was Petr Molner, RGIA, arch.468, inv.1, act.4037, fol.160 *verso*.
12. In his youth, Golitsyn was a page at the court of Catherine the Great and was on good terms with Grand Duke Alexander Pavlovich. He fell out of favour under Paul I and was banished from Saint Petersburg, but following the accession of Alexander I he was swiftly recalled to court. See *Entsiklopedikcheskii slovar'. Pod red. Andreevskogo I.E.* (Saint Petersburg, 1893), vol.9, p.50.

Emperor Nicholas II and King George V.
Photograph. State Archive of the Russian Federation, Moscow

13. *'Za veru i vernost'.' Tri veka Rossiiskoi imperatorskoi gvardii: Katalog vystavki* exh. cat. (Saint Petersburg, 2003), No.2, pp.27–8.

14. Ibid., p.105.

15. The workshop was located at No. 10 Troitskaya Street in Saint Petersburg.

16. Shepelev, L.E., *Chinovnyi mir Rossii* (Saint Petersburg, 1999), p.421.

17. The tradition of describing and representing the events relating to the accession of Russian sovereigns originated in the second half of the seventeenth century during the rule of Tsar Alexey Mikhailovich, when a manuscript illustrated with highly coloured miniatures was issued, entitled 'A Book About the Election of Tsar Mikhail Feodorovich'. Throughout the eighteenth and nineteenth centuries, several printed and engraved publications were dedicated to the theme of the coronation of Russian Emperors as an event of the greatest State and political significance.

   Emperor Alexander III took the Russian throne on 1 March 1881, and on 24 January 1883 he issued a 'Proclamation on the Accomplishment of the Ceremony of Holy Coronation'. The coronation of Alexander III and his wife Maria Feodorovna was held in the original capital on 15 May 1883, with the main events taking place in the Moscow Kremlin. Emperor Alexander III's accession to the throne is recorded in this magnificent large-format illustrated publication.

   The coronation book is bound in red leather. The title *The Holy Coronation of His Majesty Emperor Alexander III* is printed on the front cover inside a wide ornamental gold frame above the image of a double-headed eagle beneath a crown and the date 'the 15th day of May' and '1883'. Images of the State Regalia – the Imperial crown, orb and sceptre – are printed in gold on the leather spine. The book contains 60 pages, of which pages 3–60 consist of text illustrated with headpieces, tail-pieces, ornamented initials and numerous images in the form of chromolithographs, lithographs and engravings on wood. There are 25 full-page chromolithographs depicting the main events of the coronation festivities, portraits of the reigning individuals, and images of the coronation attributes. These chromolithographs are made from drawings of famous Russian artists, including I. Kramskoy, the Makovsky brothers, V. Vereshchagin, V. Surikov and V. Polenov.

18. Aksel'rod, V.I. and Bulankova, L.P., *Anichkov dvorets – legendy i byli* (Saint Petersburg, 1996), p.82.

19. F. Rauser was tailor to His Imperial Majesty and His Imperial Highness Grand Duke Vladimir Alexandrovich. His studio was based in Saint Petersburg 'at No. 9 Bol'shaya Sadovaya Street, between Ital'yanska Street and Nevsky Prospekt', RGIA, arch.1340, inv.1, act.284, pp.86, 131.

20. GARF, arch.660, inv.1, act.42, fol.161 *verso*.

21. Mosolov, A.A., *Pri dvore poslednego imperatora: Zapiski nachal'nika kantselyarii ministra dvora* (Saint Petersburg, 1992), p.85.

22. Massi, S., *Pavlovsk. Zhizn' russkogo dvortsa* (Saint Petersburg, 1990), pp.182–3.

23. GARF, arch.660, inv.1, act.42, fol.161 *verso*.

24. GARF, arch.146, inv.1, act.1115, fol.265 *verso*.

25. Nikolai Ivanovich Nordenstrem was a merchant of the second guild and supplier to the Heir Tsesarevich Nikolai Alexandrovich from 25 May 1894; his workshop and shop selling military attire were located at No.46 Nevsky Prospekt in Saint Petersburg, 'opposite Gostinnyi Dvor in the house of General Sutgov.' Uniforms were ordered at N.I. Nordenstrem's workshop for Alexander III and from 1877 for his Imperial Highness Nikolai Alexandrovich. On 25 May 1894, N.I. Nordenstrem was appointed supplier to His Imperial Majesty. RGIA, arch.468, inv.42, act.1923, fols.2, 9, 234 *verso*; arch.472, act.40, fol.231; arch.1340, inv.1, act.284, fol.14.

26. Trubetskoi, V.S., *Zapiski kirasira* (Moscow, 1991), p.157.

27. The shop was located at No.4 Vladimirskaya Street in Saint Petersburg. The firm was founded in 1853 by the Saint Petersburg merchant and manufacturer of officers' accoutrements Vasili Skosyrev; from 1860, 'following the closure of the workshop of Bitner, who had previously held the privilege,' it supplied 'items for the personal wardrobe of His Majesty', RGIA, arch.468, inv.8, act.195, fol.2.

28. Inspector and control technician of the Ministry of the Imperial Court.

29 Work on the order was undertaken within the firm by technical master S.K. Lipinskii and artists A.I. Maslennikov, A.I. Sokolov and A.G. Nesterov. The trusted Sapozhnikovy firm was rewarded for 'thrift and carefulness in fulfilment of the order,' as were the director of the silk-weaving mill I. Kukin and the weavers P.A. Burov, V. Stepanov and S.S. Slavinov.

30. The workshop, which belonged to Olga Nikolaevna Bul'benkova, was located at apartment 67, No.8 Moika Street in Saint Petersburg.

31. One of the merchants trading under this company name in 1896 was V.G. Sapozhnikov, a manufacture-counsellor of the first guild from Moscow. The firm's shops were located on the corner of Red Square and Il'inka Street in Moscow and at the Nizhegorodskaya Yarmarka in Nizhnyi Novgorod, one of Russia's main trading cities.

32. The owner of the firm was titular counsellor F.K. Martini, supplier to the Imperial Court. His workshops were located at No.16 Bol'shaya Morskaya Street in Saint Petersburg, RGIA, arch.472, inv.64, act.3, fols.316, 357.

33. Shtumpf succeeded Pel' as master bootmaker at the court of His Imperial Majesty and the court of His Imperial Highness the Heir Tsesarevich. His workshop was located at No.5 Gorokhovaya Street in Saint Petersburg, RGIA, arch.468, inv.8, act.194, fols.264–5.

34. The shop operated out of apartments No.32–4 in the Catholic Church building on Nevsky Prospekt in Saint Petersburg, RGIA, arch.468, inv.8, acts.194, 272.

35. The factory was located at No.6 Nevsky Prospekt in Saint Petersburg, RGIA, arch.472, inv.64, act.31, fol.12 *verso*.

36. The firm was located on Nevsky Prospekt in Saint Petersburg, 'near the Police Bridge'. RGIA, arch.472, inv.64, act.31, fols.4, 12 (*verso*).

37. RGIA, arch. 472, inv.64, act.3, fol.264; act.34, fol.83.

38. RGIA, arch. 468, inv. 8, act.194, fols.254, 287–9.

39. RGIA, arch.472, inv.65, act.104a, fol.321.

40. Moskovskie sovremennye letopisi: perepiska izdatelya 'Otechestvennykh zapisok', *Otechestvennye zapiski* (1826), no.27, pp.288–9.

THE WARDROBE OF EMPEROR PETER II

1. 'Pis'ma o Rossii v Ispaniyu duka de-Liriya', *Osmnadtsatyi vek. Istoricheskii sbornik* (Moscow, 1869), p.59.

2. *Dnevnik kamer-yunkera Berkhgol'tsa, vedennyi im v Rossii v tsarstvovanie Petra Velikogo, s 1721 po 1725 god.* (Moscow, 1858), pt.2, p.136.

3. 'Pis'ma o Rossii v Ispaniyu duka de-Liriya', p.59.

4. *'Za veru i vernost', Tri veka Rossiiskoi imperatorskoi gvardii: Katalog vystavki*, exh. cat. (Saint Petersburg, 2003), part 2, p.17; Mertsalova, M.N., *Kostyum raznykh vremen i narodov* (Saint Petersburg, 2001), vols.3 and 4, pp.31, 37.

5. Anisimov, E.V., *Rossiya bez Petra: 1725–1740* (Saint Petersburg, 1994), pp.157–8.

6. Kirsanova, R.M., *Russkii kostyum i byt XVIII–XIX vekov* (Moscow, 2002), p.15.

7. Moiseenko, E.Yu., 'Opis' garderoba A.D. Menshikova', *Trudy Gosudarstvennogo Ermitazha* (Leningrad, 1974), vol.15, p.102.

8. *Polnoe sobranie zakonov Rossiiskoi imperii* (Saint Petersburg, 1830), vol.5, no.3089, p.496.

9. RGADA, arch.1239, inv.3, pt.78, act.34739, fols.15, 63, 105, 8, 36, 49, 57, 84.

10. RGADA, arch. 14, act. 79 (1), fols 2, 8, 32 *verso*, 49, 53.

WEAPONS AND JEWELLERY

1. 'Puteshestvie Uil'yama Koksa. 1778 g.', *Russkaya starina* (Saint Petersburg, 1877), vol.19, p.30.

2. RGIA, arch.468, inv.44, act.1410, fols.14–14 *verso*.

3. Otdel rukopisnykh, pechatnykh i graficheskikh fondov (Department of Manuscripts, Prints and Graphics of the Moscow Kremlin Museums; hereafter ORPGF), arch.20, inv. of acts from 1922, act.5, fol.80; arch.1, inv.3, act.13, fol.223 *verso*.

4. *Zapiski imperatritsy Ekateriny II* (Moscow, 1989), p.372.

5. *Khudozhestvennye sokrovishcha Rossii* (Saint Petersburg, 1904), p.104.

6. The palace was located at No.21 Fontanka River Embankment in Saint Petersburg. It operated as the Museum of Daily Life from 1919 to 1925, when it was closed down and the collection was dispersed.

7. Konopleva, M., 'Dvortsy-muzei. Osobnyak Shuvalovykh', *Sredi kollektsionerov* (Moscow, Jul–Aug 1922), p.31.

8. ORPGF, Muzeev Moskovskogo Kremlya , arch.1, inv.3, act.15, fols.204–204 *verso*.

COURT LIVERY

1. Paleolog, M., *Tsarskaya Rossiya nakanune revolyutsii* (Moscow, 1991), p.33.

2. The models used were the vestments of the Prussian Order of the Black Eagle, the French Order of the Holy Spirit and the British Order of the Garter.

3. 'Memuary grafini Golovinoi', *Istoricheskaya biblioteka Sfinksa* (Moscow, 1911), vol.1, p.182.

4. 'Doneseniya i drugie bymagi angliiskikh poslov, poslannikov i rezidentov pri russkom dvore s 1728 goda po 1733 god', *Sbornik Imperatorskogo russkogo istoricheskogo obshchestva* (Saint Petersburg, 1889), vol.66, p.228.

5. Mosolov, A.A. *Pri dvore poslednego imperatora: Zapiski nachal'nika kantselyarii ministra dvora* (Leningrad, 1992), p.90.

FANCY DRESS

1. RGIA, arch.476, inv.1, act.1484, fols.128–128 *verso*.

2. From the diaries of V.A. Telyakovskii, Gosudarstvennyi tsentral'nyi teatral'nyi muzei imeni A.A. Bakhrushina (The Bakhrushkin State Central Museum of Theatrical Art), arch.280, act.1254, fol.3225.

3. A mixed spectacle was scheduled for this date consisting of the second act of the opera *Boris Godunov*, starring F. Shalyapin; the play *The Russian Benefactress*, starring M. Savina; and the third act of the ballet *La Bayadère*, starring A. Pavlova and T. Karsavina.

4. RGIA, arch.1088, inv.2, act.731, fol.53. The diary refers to the following titles: Savvaitov, P.I., *Opisanie starinnykh tsarskikh ytvarei, odezhd, oruzhiya, ratnykh dospekhov i konskogo pribora* (Saint Petersburg, 1865), 1st ed., (Saint Petersburg, 1896), 2nd ed.; Zabelin, I.E., *Domashnii byt russkogo naroda v XVI–XVII st.: V 2 t.* (Moscow, 1862–9); and Viskovatov, A.V., *Istoricheskoe opisanie odezhdy I vooruzheniya rossiiskikh voisk* (Saint Petersburg, 1841–62).

5. George, Grand Duchess of Russia, *A Romanov Diary: The Autobiography of H.I. and R.H. Grand Duchess George* (New York, 1988), p.102.

6. From the recollections of V. Dolgorukaya. See Princess Varvara Dolgoruky, *Au Temps des Troikas – Russia 1886–1919* (Paris, 1978).

7. He married twice, first in 1648 and then in 1671.

8. RGIA, arch.652, inv.2, act.4, fol.12.

9. George, Grand Duchess of Russia, *A Romanov Diary: The Autobiography of H.I. and R.H. Grand Duchess George* (New York, 1988), p.102.

10. RGIA, arch.652, inv.2, act.4, fol.11.

11. It effectively eclipsed the last ball that actually took place at the Imperial Court, which was the Bol'shoi Nikolaevsky ball in January 1904.

12. Voeikov, V.N., *S Tsarem i bez Tsarya. Vospominaniya poslednego dvortsovogo komendanta Gosudarya Imperatora Nikolaya II* (Moscow, 1994), p.25.

13. From the diary of Grand Duchess Kseniya Aleksandrovna, GARF, arch.662, act.18, fol.228.

14. From the diary of I.A. Vsevolozhskii, RGIA, arch.652, inv.2, act.4, fol.35.

15. RGIA, arch.468, inv.32, act.1648, fol.47.

16. RGIA, arch.525, inv.3, act.15, fol.105.

17. GARF, arch.601, inv.1, act.1712, fols.27–27 *verso*.

18. For example, the V&A acquired some for the museum collection in 1972.

Bibliography

Amelekhina, S.A., 'Koronatsiya Ekateriny I', *Petr Velikii i Moskva: Katalog vystavki. GTG* (Moscow, 1998), pp.168–171

Amelekhina, S.A., 'Sostav i osobennosti formirovaniya kompleksa koronatsionnykh kostyumov rossiiskikh monarkhov v Oruzheinoi palate', *Filimonovskie chteniya* (Moscow, 2004), 1, pp.225–33

Amelekhina, S.A., 'K voprosu o koronatsionnom kostyume imperatora Pavla I', *Filimonovskie chteniya* (Moscow, 2004), 2, pp.202–9

Amelekhina, S.A. and Gafifullin, R.R., 'Koronatsionnye kostyumy imperatora Nikolaya II i imperatritsy Aleksandry Feodorovny', *Problemy izucheniya pamyatnikov dukhovnoi i material'noi kul'tury* (2000), 3, pp.102–7

Amelekhina, S.A. and Gafifullin, R.R., 'Ordenskii kostyum pri Rossiiskom imperatorskom dvore', *Pinakoteka* (Moscow, 1998), no.5, pp.5–15

Andreev, A.I, 'Petr I v Anglii v 1698', *Petr Velikii* (Moscow, Leningrad, 1947), pp.63–103

Delpierre, M., *Dress in France in the 18th Century* (Paris, 1997)

Dukes, P., *A History of Russia c.882–1996* (London, 1998)

Gafifullin, R.R., Amelekhina, S.A., Moiseenko, E.Yu. et al., *Kostyumirovannyi bal v Zimnem dvortse. Issledovaniya, dokumenty, materialy* (Moscow, 2003), vol.2

Hughes, L., *Russia in the Age of Peter the Great* (New Haven, London, 1998)

Madariaga, I. D., *Russia in the Age of Catherine the Great* (New Haven, London, 1981)

Kogan, I.I., 'Moskovskie shelkovye fabriki pervoi poloviny XVIII v.' *Staraya Moskva. Stat'i po istorii Moskvy v XVII–XIX v.* (Moscow, 1929), coll.1, pp.127–44

Likhacheva, O.O., 'Rossiiskie prazdniki v istorii kul'tury Peterburga I chetverty XIX veka', abstract from Cand. Sci. (History) dissertation (Saint Petersburg, 1977)

Moiseenko, E.Yu., 'Mastera-portnye 'nemetskogo plat'ya' v Rossii i ikh raboty', *Trudy Gosudarstvennogo Ermitazha* (Leningrad, 1974), vol.15, pp.142–50

Pylyaev, M.I., 'Epokha rytsarskikh karuselei i allegoricheskikh maskaradov v Rossii', *Istoricheskii vestnik* (Saint Petersburg, 1885), vol.21, pp.309–39

Samonin, S.Yu., 'Voennyi kostyum v Rossii XVIII-nachala XX veka', *Kostyum v Rossii XV–nachala XX veka. Iz sobraniya GIM (Gosudarstvennogo Istoricheskogo muzeya)* (Moscow, 2000), pp.173–227

Saunders, D., *Russia in the Age of Reaction and Reform, 1801–1881* (London, 1992)

Shepelev, L.E., *Chinovnyi mir Rossii. XVIII–nachalo XX v.* (Saint Petersburg, 1999)

Thornton, P., *Baroque and Rococo Silks* (London, 1965)

Wortman, R.S., *Scenarios of Power Myth and Ceremony in Russian Monarchy from Peter the Great to the Abduction of Nicholas II* (Princeton, 2004)

Further Reading

Arch, N., and J. Marschner, *Splendour at Court. Dressing for Royal Occasions since 1700* (London, 1987)

Gorguet Ballesteros, P. (ed.), *Modes et Miroirs. La France et la Hollande au temps des Lumières* (Paris, 2005)

Mansel, P., *Dressed to Rule* (New Haven and London, 2005)

Rangström, L., *Lions of Fashion: Male fashion of the 16th, 17th, 18th centuries* (Stockholm, 2003)

Ribeiro, A., *Dress in Eighteenth Century Europe 1715–1789* (New Haven and London, 2002)

Rothstein, N., *Silk Designs of the Eighteenth Century* (London, 1991)

Index